TAND

Curry Cookbook

TANDOORI
Curry Cookbook

PAT CHAPMAN

PIATKUS

© 1995 Pat Chapman

First published in 1995 by
Judy Piatkus (Publishers) Limited
5 Windmill Street, London W1P 1HF

First mass market paperback edition 1997
The moral right of the author has been asserted

*A catalogue record for this book
is available from the British Library*

ISBN 0-7499-1741-5

Design and artwork by Suzanne Perkins
Illustration of tandoori oven and map by Dick Vine

Cover photograph by James Murphy shows Meat Tikka (page 31), Chicken Tikka
Pieces (page 52) and Tandoori Chicken Joints (page 55)

Typeset by Selwood Systems, Midsomer Norton
Printed and bound in Great Britain by
Mackays of Chatham plc, Chatham, Kent

Contents

Preface

This book started life as *Tandoori and Tikka Dishes*, a small 60 page hardback containing 60 recipes.

By popular demand Pat Chapman has developed and expanded that book to give more information, more history, more background and above all, more recipes, in particular about the recent development from the curry houses – favourite curries whose starting point is the tandoori oven.

All this and much more is in this book, all written in Pat Chapman's easy to follow, do-it-at-home style.

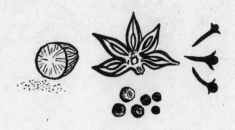

Foreword

Britain's first recorded invasion took place 2,000 years ago when Julius Caesar spearheaded a highly sophisticated occupation that made England into the most distant part of the Roman empire, and which lasted 400 years. The subsequent invasions from the Saxons, Danes and Vikings were rather less civilised but they too left their indelible marks on the nation. The Norman conquest of 1066 was the final invasion to succeed and despite attempts from the Spanish, French and Germans we have remained a stubborn, insular, wealthy, arrogant, defiant, self critical, conservative nation, highly resistant to change, and very suspicious of it.

These qualities resulted in the establishment of the world's most successful and comprehensive empire and a reputation of invincibility and immortality. Our culinary reputation was never placed into such high echelons, indeed most nations thought British food to be bland and totally unworthy of tasting. Both reputations were short of the mark. Our empire was not invincible nor immortal, and our indigenous food can be exquisite when kept out of the hands of canteen caterers and mass producers. However, until just a few decades ago, garlic was an ingredient which was hard to obtain and which appeared in no British food, and the few spices we used were the likes of cloves, pepper, mustard and caraway.

It may be because of this gap, that the arrival and growth of ethnic restaurants, especially curry and tandoori houses, has been so spectacularly rapid nationwide. In 1946, just after the war, there were six Indian restaurants in the whole of Great Britain. Only one, **Veeraswamy** in Regent Street, had any mention of tandoori. On their menu dating from the early 1950s, *'Tunduri Chicken'* cost 2/6d (12½ pence in today's money), which was considered expensive then. But they had no tandoori oven – and the trend which was to sweep the country had not yet begun.

Exactly who brought the first tandoor to Britain is a matter of great debate. I know several restaurateurs who claim it was them. Des Sarda, owner of the excellent **Rajdoot** group in Bristol, Birmingham, Manchester and Dublin, says he was first in 1966, when he opened the **Tandoori of Chelsea**, 153, Fulham Road, SW3. Messrs Gai and Lamba of the **Gaylord** restaurants in London's W1 say it was them. Mohindra Kaul of **The Viceroy of India**, NW1 is a contender, and there are others. All of these restaurants were founded in the 1960s, and all are upmarket, smart establishments, which set new trends for others to follow.

It would be the 1970s before the trend began in earnest. By now there were some 1,500 to 2,000 curry houses up and down the nation, and most were Bangladeshi run. Bangladesh was by then independent of Pakistan (where tandoori cooking originated, see page 5) and is some 1,400 miles (2,240km) distant. Most Bangladeshi curry house owners had not a clue about how to cook tandoori food let alone what a tandoor was. No such thing existed at the time in Bangladesh.

Yet within a few years, nearly every curry house nationwide had become a tandoori restaurant. Many did not even possess a tandoor. Yet they all felt it essential to be able to offer tandoori food.

And they were quite right, of course. Tandoori food is unique, it is wonderfully tasty, low in calories, high in nutrients, and it is a great way to introduce a first-timer to the curry house.

By 1994, of the 8,000 curry houses in the UK, over 95 per cent describe themselves as tandoori restaurants. There are now nearly as many such establishments in the British Isles as there are fish and chip shops or chemists. And there are far more here than in the whole of India.

Over the last 20 years, from a starting point of virtually zero to near saturation of the nation, an invasion has finally succeeded after 900 years – the tandoori invasion. It is total, peaceful, popular and probably irreversible. It too has left an indelible mark on the nation. Its effect on the indigenous population has been transmogrifying. We are a nation of tandoori addicts.

Food is arguably the most successful route to multi-racial integration, and if Britain's empire achieved anything it has led to a remarkable conversion of the British palate. We still adore our roasts and our fry-ups, our fish and chips and our steak and kidney puds, but we have the added advantage of access to a wealth of extra choice available from our ethnic restaurants, our supermarkets and our delicatessens.

The tandoori invasion of Britain is one of the world's outstanding culinary success stories. And it is a story which has not reached its conclusion yet. Statistics reveal that over 60 per cent of the population enjoy tandoori dishes regularly. But they also show that a stubborn 8 per cent have not tried tandoori, or curry, or Chinese, or indeed any ethnic food. They detest garlic, though they are unlikely to have ever eaten it and nothing, they say, will convert them.

The interesting facts are that tandoori is immensely popular with an increasingly younger age group, and of the remaining 30 per cent (who have never, or rarely, tasted its delights) fortunately there are thousands converted daily. By my reckoning the invasion and my job will not be complete until 100 per cent enjoy the delights of tandoori food as a regular part of their diet. As a user of this book you will almost certainly already be a convert, and I hope its contents will enable you to explore possibilities to greater depths. In particular, I hope you'll cook from this book, for your friends and guests. There is no better introduction to the food of the Indian subcontinent than tandoori food. I pray you'll make some converts yourself.

Pat Chapman
Haslemere

Introduction

WHAT ARE TANDOORI AND TIKKA?

Tandoori cooking is a unique method of cooking food (meat, poultry, seafood or vegetables) over a charcoal heat source, controlled inside a purpose-built 'oven' called the **tandoor**. The food is coated with a thick sauce comprising of yoghurt and spices, and left to marinade for some time to allow the flavours to penetrate the meat or chicken etc and to tenderise it.

The marinated food, such as a whole chicken, leg of lamb or whole fish, is then threaded on to long **skewers** and placed in the tandoor. The tandoor's design results in an efficient stream of very hot air flowing past the food and cooking it. The item can also be cut into small cubes (**tikkas**) prior to marinating. A further variation, the **sheek kebab**, requires the meat to be pounded or ground with spices. No marination takes place before the meat is moulded on to the skewer and cooked in the tandoor. A particular type of flat leavened bread **naan** or **nan** is also tandoori cooked and is the traditional accompaniment, along with fresh chutneys, salad and lemon wedges.

Tandoori cooking achieves its exquisite tastes from a combination of the marinade and the flavour that the tandoori heated charcoal imparts into the food. And I have to admit that you will not achieve exactly the same flavour with a conventional oven, although it will come somewhere close. Alternatively you can cook many of the recipes over barbecue coals. Domestic sized tandoors are available and serious tandoori addicts use them with great success at home. If you feel that you would like to obtain one, I give information on how to obtain and operate them on page 10.

Most people, however, wish to achieve good results using their normal cooking appliance, so all my recipes are written for the grill or main oven.

A LITTLE HISTORY

From the moment prehistoric man learned to harness fire, he cooked the wild animals and fowl he hunted by suspending their carcasses over a slow fire.

Dr KT Achaya is a scientific researcher specialising in the food oils and nutrition of India. He is also a food historian and author, and in his recent book, *Indian Food, A Historical Companion*, published by the Delhi Oxford University Press, he has this to say about the origins of cooking: 'When and where the use of fire originated is not known. Suspending an animal high above fire is still practised by primitive peoples, not to cook meat, but to prevent it from putrefying too quickly. Sparks from spontaneous friction, or even forest fires could have led man to the concept of roasting meat directly on a flame, or on hot ashes or embers. The Peking Cave in China, which was in use 500,000 years ago, shows evidence of the use of fire for roasting and cooking meat.'

The transition from hunting to herding began about 12,000 years ago and gradually resulted in greater sophistication in the cookery department. By 2500 BC there were four literate independent civilisations, those of China, Egypt, Mesopotamia (settled around the valley areas now called the Levant, around the rivers Tigris and Euphrates) and of the Indus Valley. The latter civilisation extended for some 800 miles (1,280 km), north westwards along the course of the river Indus (now in today's Pakistan) from its estuary at the Arabian sea to the mountain ranges which include the Karakorams and Himalayas.

Extensive remains of towns and cities, principal of which were Harappa and Mohenjodaro, had remained buried, undisturbed, deep under yards of top soil since their decline some 3,000 years ago. Their discovery this century classes as one of the most exciting archaeological finds ever, enabling a great many of the 'missing links' of early civilisation to be filled in. Amongst these finds were a number in the culinary department, including vast sophisticated granaries and food warehouses. Huge pottery jars containing carbonised wheat, barley, chickpeas and chana (gram) lentils have been excavated. Large platforms for pounding grain indicate that flour was made. Carbonised spices such as mustard, caraway, sesame and cloves, and grinding stones of all shapes and sizes, indicate that the use of spices was widespread over 5,000 years ago. Charred bones (mainly of cattle, mutton, tortoises and fish) indicate that what was eaten was roasted or grilled. Few poultry remains exist and it appears not to have figured largely if at all in the diet of the time.

Dr Achaya says, 'Baking, called *putapaka*, is not a common style of Indian cooking. Many circular ovens (clay) have been found at Indus Valley sites. Some are extremely large and have a firing section placed below the ground; these were almost certainly used for firing and glazing large clay objects, for bread-making, or even for metallurgy. Smaller mud-plastered ovens with a side opening are in evidence at Kalibangan, very closely resembling the present-day tandoors.'

Parallel evidence has been uncovered in Egypt. Indeed archaeologists are certain that it was ancient Egypt who invented the leavening (rising) process and baking of bread. It is probable, therefore, that they also invented the oven. Called the 'tonir', the ancient Egyptian oven was hemispherical and made of clay, with a side tunnel large enough to allow bread discs to be slid into the main oven. Before long much of the ancient world had learned to make leavened bread in the form of flat loaves. Bread became the staff of life and one of the world's staples. It was not the only staple, as is clearly demonstrated in India, where rice has grown in the greater part of the sub-continent for thousands of years.

Indian Economic historian Professor KN Chaudhuri in his book *Trade and Civilisation in the Indian Ocean* (Cambridge University Press) makes the distinction between the two Indian cultures at the time of the rise of Islam, around 7–800 AD. One was rice-eating; the other wheat-eating. 'Wheat was a dry crop which needed selective irrigation if the winter rain was insufficient or irregular. It was the preferred food in the Middle East, North India, Central Asia, and the northern frontier districts of China. Various kinds of bread from wheat flour revealed the national or ethnic identity of the baker and his customers. The huge flat loaves eaten by Turks, Persians, and Afghans were baked in large ovens. Large ovens were the tell-tale signs of low winter temperatures and the presence of high mountains. In India bread was rolled thin and cooked over open wood fires or fried in oil.' Clearly this latter observation refers to unleavened Indian breads such as chupatti, parathas and puris. The 'huge flat loaves' are the *pitta* of Turkey and the *nane lavash* of Persia. Nane (pronounced narn) evolved into the naan of Afghanistan. Even today you will find more varieties of naan breads in Kabul than anywhere else. These include the 'standard' naan (see page 111). You will also find the *naan-e-nakhooni*, whose surface is indented with the impression of nails, *naan-e-panjagi* decorated with a series of depressions made with finger tips, *naan-parakki* long, thin and crisp, and *naan roghani* kneaded with ghee. (Recipes for all of the exciting naan variants appear in Chapter 8.)

The word *kebab* or *kabab*, *kebob* etc, appears in many ancient languages including Persian, Arabic and Turkish, but exactly who invented the kebab is a subject for debate.

In her book *The Legendary Cuisine of Persia*, Margaret Shaida attributes the origin of the kebab to Iran from where it, 'spread across the Middle East in the seventh and eighth centuries.' But when did this technique pass into the sub-continent of India? Margaret Shaida believes it was the Moghul emperors with their Persian ancestry who were responsible: 'The court language of the Moghul (the Persian for Mongol) emperors of Delhi was Persian, their culture Iranian, and their religion Islam. Their food, of course, was wholly Persian. The Moghuls took with them not only the traditions and language of the Persian court but also those of the Persian kitchen. The direct influence can be easily identified in many Indian dishes today. The Persian bread (*nan*) made with yeast and baked in an oven (*tanoor*) took India by storm when it was first introduced there. It was a light yet substantial alternative to the unleavened and fried breads of the subcontinent. Another, equally ancient Persian word is *tikeh*, meaning a little piece.'

It is an attractive theory. However the Indus Valley civilisation predates the Persian empire by many centuries. What is certain is that the side entry oven, (Egypt's tonir and Persia's tanoor) was also used in Afghanistan and the Indus Valley for bread making long before the coming of Islam.

The demise of the Indus Valley civilisation (around 1000 BC) led to a long period of 'dark ages' where no records were kept, no cities were built and no remains were left to be uncovered. Although they lived in isolation, the tribes of India's north west evidently retained their tonir/tanoor ovens.

We do not know how and when that oven turned through 90 degrees to become a sphere with a narrow-necked opening at the top – the *tandoor*. The charred bones from the ancient Indus Valley cannot tell us whether the meat was marinated or indeed whether it was oven cooked. Sadly, no such evidence can survive for thousands of years in the form of remains.

It was the isolation of these mountains which caused the tandoor and its cooking style to remain unique to that north-western wheat growing area. We can only speculate that the marination of meat in yoghurt and spices slowly evolved during that period.

It is entirely conceivable that it was the Moghuls who perfected Indian tandoori cooking, as they did with their entire range of dishes such as korma, roghan gosht, biriani and kofta dishes. But it is unlikely that they invented it. It is much more probable that early Turk, Persian and Arab Moslem invaders of the eighth and ninth centuries brought kebabs and charcoal cooking with them as they came through the passes of Persia, and Afghanistan, such as the famous Khyber Pass. They became established in the rugged and mountainous tribal areas of what is now called The North West Frontier in Pakistan and to evolve over the next few hundred years into the delicious cooking style we know today.

The *shish kabab* became the *sheek kebab*, spicy ground meat on a skewer, *tikeh*, the little piece, became *tikka*, a small cube of meat or poultry. The marinades became highly spiced and colourful, and yoghurt was incorporated to improve the marination process, particularly to assist with the tenderising of the meat or poultry, which were usually very tough. The *nane* became the *naan* bread.

The Moghul dynasty reached its peak during the sixteenth and seventeenth centuries. There is ample written evidence to prove that the tandoori cooking style had been established in the emperors' main fortress courts of Agra, Delhi, Kashmir and Lahore. I have personally met a young chef at the *Mughal Sheraton Hotel Agra*, who specialises only in sheek kebabs and naan bread making. He was taught the process by his father, who was taught the process by *his* father and so on backwards. He claims that generations ago his ancestors, who have always lived in Agra, were kebab and bread chefs to the emperors. (The story is the same with stone masons, jewellers and carpenters, prostitutes, boatmen and money lenders, all of whom still live in the village adjacent to the Taj Mahal.) And why should I doubt him?

The demise of the Moghuls in the eighteenth century must have come as a shock to such artisans as these. With their patrons gone, replaced by the puritanical British, there was little demand for any of these, let alone kebab chefs. Tandoori technology and know-how, simple though it was, almost faded out altogether.

Fortunately for the world, however, tandoori cooking survived where it had begun – in the North West Frontier area. Following the partition of India and Pakistan in 1947, one successful Indian Hindu restaurateur, fearing Moslem violence, closed his Tandoori restaurant in Lahore and moved to Delhi. Strangely enough tandoori cooking was virtually unknown in post partition India. The tradition for eating out in restaurants was confined to tourists and adventurous Indians in those days (it is still not a widely accepted activity there), but the *Moti Mahal* immediately became one of Delhi's talking points, with its flavourful colourful Tandoori food.

From their humble beginnings Indian restaurants began a growth pattern which, as I have mentioned on page x, is showing no sign of stopping. The arrival of the tandoor in the 1970s helped greatly to establish the curry and tandoori house as a British institution. And it is a phenomenon which is repeating itself world-wide. The same thing is happening in America, Canada, Australasia and South Africa. Tandoori restaurants are becoming hugely popular in the Middle East, Singapore, Hong Kong and Japan.

Chicken tikka masala is by far the most popular main course dish at the curry restaurant, with chicken tikka/tandoori the most popular starter. And the curry houses, never slow to exploit a good thing, now offer such remarkable combinations as, for example, chicken tikka dhansak, or tandoori meat bhoona masala, or sag aloo roghan josh tandoori. I have included some of these dishes in this book.

Tandoori and tikka products do not stop at the restaurant. They are to be found at the supermarket and delicatessen. Fresh, frozen and chilled tandoori and tikka ready meals, canned and bottled tandoori and tikka sauces and pastes and dry mixes abound. But it does not stop even there. The most popular sandwich is now

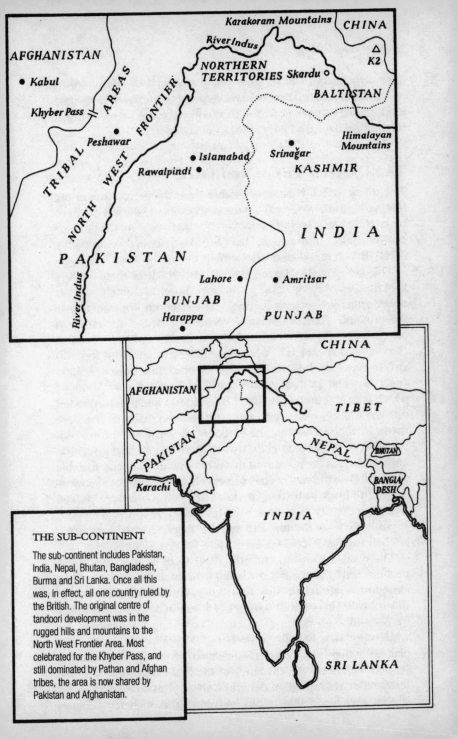

Karakoram Mountains
CHINA

River Indus

AFGHANISTAN

NORTHERN
TERRITORIES   Skardu

K2

Kabul

Khyber Pass

BALTISTAN

TRIBAL AREAS

NORTH WEST FRONTIER

Peshawar

Himalayan
Mountains

Islamabad

Srinagar

Rawalpindi

KASHMIR

INDIA

PAKISTAN

River Indus

Lahore

Amritsar

PUNJAB

Harappa

PUNJAB

CHINA

AFGHANISTAN

TIBET

PAKISTAN

NEPAL

BHUTAN

BANGLA
DESH

Karachi

INDIA

THE SUB-CONTINENT

The sub-continent includes Pakistan,
India, Nepal, Bhutan, Bangladesh,
Burma and Sri Lanka. Once all this
was, in effect, all one country ruled by
the British. The original centre of
tandoori development was in the
rugged hills and mountains to the
North West Frontier Area. Most
celebrated for the Khyber Pass, and
still dominated by Pathan and Afghan
tribes, the area is now shared by
Pakistan and Afghanistan.

SRI LANKA

filled with chicken tikka, and you can even buy tikka topped pizzas, and tandoori-flavoured mayonnaise. Chicken tikka lasagne is advertised by a major frozen food company and I've even heard of tandoori flavoured pepperoni meat sticks!

TANDOORI TECHNOLOGY

The magic which is tandoori comes from the ingredients in the marinade, and of course from the tandoor oven which is purpose built to cook tandoori to perfection. As we have seen, the tandoor evolved many centuries ago. I have heard it described as 'simplicity itself'. In fact this is an overstatement.

The tandoor is a large pottery tub, which is more or less spherical with an opening in the top. More accurately it is an oblate-spheroid (or egg shaped). The diagram opposite shows the principle. The professional version as used in the tandoori restaurant averages 3 feet (nearly 1 metre) high and 2 feet 6 inches (75 cm) in diameter. The opening at the top is about one foot (30 cm) in diameter. It is hand 'thrown' in one continuous operation (no mean feat in itself) from a special blend of clay, some of which is only found in the East. Bangladeshi jute is incorporated into the walls (which are about 2 inches/5 cm thick) to reinforce them. In village Pakistan, the tandoors are buried in the ground, the earth being packed tightly around them, to give heat insulation and stability. In the restaurant this is not practical (or comfortable to operate) so the clay oven is securely housed in a square enclosure of fire brick insulation blocks. The open cavities are packed with high density glass-fibre wool insulation. A concrete top and ceramic tiles on the top and outside faces, creates a hygienic kitchen appliance, cold on the outside yet very hot inside.

The oven is supplied unfired. (After three or four uses it has become fired.) A small draw hole at the base can be opened or closed to create an air flow. Charcoal is the traditional fuel, and this is loaded in to about 6 inches (15 cm) in depth. It must then be allowed $2\frac{1}{2}$–3 hours to reach its operating temperature, by which time it is literally white hot (700°F/370°C). This extraordinarily high temperature is achieved by minimising heat loss (which maximises the efficiency of the fuel combustion), by the totally effective insulation described above. It is a property of the special clay blend that it can withstand this high temperature

Tandoori oven installation: cross section

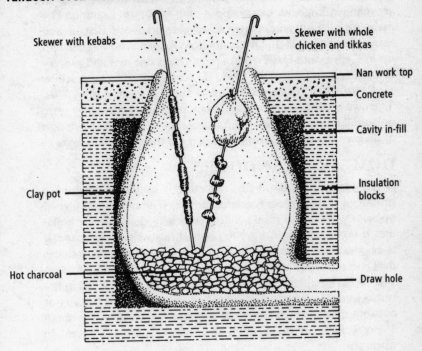

Skewer with kebabs

Skewer with whole chicken and tikkas

Nan work top

Concrete

Cavity in-fill

Clay pot

Insulation blocks

Hot charcoal

Draw hole

without cracking, and the coals can be allowed to extinguish and go cold between usages with no shrinkage.

The only other implements a tandoori chef requires are a metal lid to cover the oven's opening to retain heat while the oven is 'at rest', and several long skewers. These are about 3 feet (90 cm) in length and often have a square profile of about $\frac{1}{2}$ inch (1.25 cm) square. (Round skewers would cause the food to rotate on them when turned.)

The tandoori boom swept across Britain in the 1970s, when every curry house claimed to be a tandoori house whether it owned a tandoor or not. But those days have gone and every restaurant usually has not one but two tandoors, one charcoal fired running at temperatures of up to 700°F/370°C, the other gas powered, operating at lower temperatures.

Despite wild claims from certain exuberant restaurant proprietors that they import their tandoors from India, most of them are made in England, in a purpose-built factory in London. The main supplier of tandoor ovens to restaurants in Britain and Europe is Shah Gulian. Originally from Armenia, he was brought up in Cyprus and qualified in architecture, fine arts and pottery at Cheltenham College in 1969. He runs an architect's practice. He designed an Indian restaurant in Hendon in the early 1970s. The owner particularly wanted a tandoor. At the time they were only available from India, so Gulian set about perfecting a design of his own. Today his team produce more than 800 each year.

DOMESTIC TANDOORS

A few years ago I asked Shah whether it would be possible to produce a small tandoor for domestic use. Within weeks he turned up with a delightful mini-version especially designed for home use. It is charcoal fired, easy to use and relatively inexpensive. It is easy to move around, can be set up anywhere and produces delicious authentic tandooris.

It comes complete on its own as a clay oven, or enclosed in fire bricks in a stainless steel wheeled box. It can be used indoors or out (but the clay must not be allowed to get wet). Its size is about 1 foot 6 inches (38 cm) high and 1 foot 3 inches (31 cm) in diameter.

It is available from Shah Gulian, The Tandoori Clay Oven Company Ltd, 164a Dukes Road, W3 OSL   Tel: 0181–896 2696.

Serious tandoori cooks are well advised to acquire one of these units. At under £300 they will soon earn their keep. The Curry Club has sold quite a number to our members. One, Dr Richard Wood of Cleveland, permanently installed one into his kitchen. This is what he says of it. 'The tandoor oven is a triumph of low technology. Everything about it is just right and works to perfection. The combustion of wood and charcoal occurs with an efficiency that I have never seen before, at high temperature with minimum heat loss. The actual cooking method is very fast baking (in fact on occasions the tandoor is almost as fast as a microwave). Food is skewered and the tip of the skewer sits in the charcoal. A good tip is to use an onion at the bottom as a stop. The heat derives from the oven environment, but also, and almost as important, much heat is conducted up the (quite thick) skewer to cook from the inside outwards. Chicken breasts or legs will cook in about 10–12 minutes. It is noticeable that bits of food near to the charcoal don't get any more browned (or charred) than bits at the top of the skewer near the mouth.'

Another Curry Club mini tandoor user, Terry Davis of Harrow, has a few important tips. '1) The amount of charcoal required is substantial, approximately 3 inches in depth. 2) It takes at least $2\frac{1}{2}$–3 hours to reach optimum cooking temperature. 3) As in ordinary barbecuing, the skewers must be oiled. 4) As the skewers are used almost vertical, small onion pieces should be used to hold the chicken in place and also for spacing, otherwise it all slides down into the fire. 5) It is necessary to have a flow of air through the tandoor to ensure that it reaches the correct temperature.'

In fact air flow is the real secret of the tandoor's success. The upper curve of the tandoor, although a feature evolved centuries ago, is in fact a perfect aerodynamic shape. It causes the hot air to accelerate on its path past the food and out of the opening. The draw hole, though appearing tiny, provides absolutely the correct amount of air into the base of the coals. It is essential to place your oven under a flue when used indoors, and to ensure that there is a sufficient air supply into the kitchen. If there isn't, the difference will be pulled down the chimney and the result will be smoke.

Wood can be used in the tandoor in place of charcoal. Dr Wood has this to say about it: 'You can use either wood or charcoal; it makes no difference. The vital thing is *Never ever use anything else, like coal etc.* Remember that everything that goes into the tandoor contributes to its inherent acquired flavour. I always throw in all garlic and ginger peelings, and anything else that is likely to add flavour. Try smelling the oven soon after it has gone out and cooled – it's distinctively sweet. And it is full of flavour. To clean simply use a vacuum cleaner through the mouth, there being little in the way of remains.'

AT THE RESTAURANT

If you haven't seen the tandoori chef at work at your favourite tandoori house, my advice is that you ask to have a look into the kitchens. Good restaurants have nothing to hide, and will welcome your interest in their work. Make sure you see the colourful marinades (the reds and oranges enhanced by food colouring) and see the long skewers being threaded and inserted into the tandoor. And don't miss the naan bread making. The chef will deftly slap it between the palms of the hands to obtain a flat disc. He then presses it directly onto the top wall of the oven. Remarkably it sticks there for the couple of minutes it takes to cook, elongating because of gravity into the familiar tear shape. Usually the chef uses a damp cloth to put the naan into place, but at one restaurant, *The Royal Naim Balti House,* 417–419, Stratford Road, Sparkhill in Birmingham, where they specialise in gigantic naans the size of an elephant's ear, they use a damp pillow to press it into place. Some restaurants have glass-fronted kitchens and you can view this work in progress.

And the whereabouts of the best tandoori restaurant in the world? In my view it's the *Bukhara* at the *Maurya Sheraton Hotel* in Delhi. Built in 1982, it seats about one hundred diners. It's always full with people queuing. Eight chefs are on view with at least six tandoori ovens in the glass kitchen. The food they turn out, with great dexterity and speed before your very eyes, is just exquisite.

ALTERNATIVE COOKING METHODS

Don't worry if you haven't got a tandoor because all the recipes in this book are written assuming the cook does not have either a tandoor or a barbecue set.

ABOUT FOOD COLOURING

Authentic tandooris and tikkas in India have always been cooked with natural colourings. Red is achieved using paprika or chilli. Deep red is from a root called *ratin jot.* Yellow comes from saffron and turmeric. There is no natural orange. I have used anatto seed powder for yellow orange and beetroot powder for deep red (see page 20). These can be obtained by post (see page 125). All these natural colours are not heat stable, so they can change colour, (becoming browner) when cooked, although the colours of the finished dishes are, in my view, perfectly attractive and natural.

The very bright reds and oranges that we are accustomed to at the tandoori house, are frankly pure boloney. They are, of course, tartrazine food dyes. Made from coal tar, they are said to have 'side effects' on a few children causing allergies and hyperactivity. However, those who wish to achieve these vibrant colours can use food colourings, in powdered form (available by post, as previously mentioned) if they wish. They do not affect the taste of the dish, but are very concentrated, so use just a tiny bit.

WHAT TO SERVE WITH TANDOORI AND TIKKA

Tandoori and tikkas are served as a starter or as a main course. Portions for a starter are smaller. Both are superb with a bed of salad. This can be much more exciting than just lettuce. There are plenty of ideas on page 29. Naan bread is almost obligatory and several versions are given between pages 111 and 116. Yoghurt-based chutney (raita) and bottled chutneys and pickles go very well. I personally adore raw onion rings and fresh onion chutney (cachumber) with tandoori dishes.

For those who want rice as well as, or instead of naan bread, there are two variations on pages 107 and 108. In my other curry books listed on page ii you will find a much greater selection of rice, bread, lentils and chutney accompaniments, most of them not hot.

DRINK

This is a personal choice. I like red wine with tandooris and curries although experts disagree about this. It should not be fine wine – a cheap and cheerful plonk will do the meal great justice in my view. Rosé, white wine, sparkling wine and real ale are also appropriate. Most lagers are too gassy, although Cobra Lager brewed in Bangalore is designed to go with curry. Non-alcoholic drinks are always acceptable.

AND FINALLY

That Tandoori has become a first class dish popular the world over, is not surprising. However, it is not only people who delight in tandoori cooking. A number of people have reported to me that their pet cats and dogs enjoy a tipple or two of tikka. But the most remarkable report of all is from Jean Judd, secretary of the National Fancy Rat Society. She keeps dozens of champion rats at her Sussex home. 'They never bite, they don't smell and they are very intelligent. They follow you around and sit on the sofa to watch TV with you.' And their favourite food? Yes you've guessed it. Miss Judd assures me that that all her rats enjoy tandooris and naan.

So for all tandoori addicts whether cats, rats, dogs, people or any other species, and for any one else who is yet to become converted, here are my 100 favourite tandoori recipes.

CHAPTER 1

The Tandoori Workshop

We have already seen that tandoori cooking requires us to marinate the main ingredient for some hours before we cook it. It is the marinade itself which imparts the 'secret' flavour to tandoori cooking.

This chapter is about the spices which we need to make the marinades, plus various other powders (masalas) and pastes which are used throughout this book.

You can, of course, buy most of the dry mixes and pastes in this chapter. There are, for example, a number of proprietory red tandoori pastes available, any of which can be used in the recipes in this book which call for red tandoori paste. I certainly do so when I have none of my own homemade in stock.

However, with a bit of forethought, and time devoted to making up your own, you'll achieve great satisfaction and you'll stamp your own personality on your cooking.

More than that, you'll greatly improve on what can be done in the factory.

To prove it, and just for fun, spend half an hour or less and make up the garam masala recipe on page 18. Now compare your own with the factory product which is in your cupboard. You'll wonder how you managed without your own – and I promise you you'll never use anything else from now on.

INGREDIENTS

Most of the fresh and dried ingredients in this book are widely available from supermarkets and delicatessens. If you do have problems obtaining any of the specialist ingredients such as ghee, coconut milk, tamarind, sizzler dishes and of course all the spices, they are available, along with much much more by mail order, see page 125.

SPICES

It is the combination of spices which makes the cooking of the sub-continent of India so special. Tandoori cooking is no exception. The spices you will need to make these recipes are not too many; neither will they cost you too much. Yet they are crucial to all which follows, so they should be cared for as if they were gold. There are some rules:

Firstly Buy in small quantities. Once their packets are opened, the spices deteriorate and eventually lose all their flavour (or essential oils). Use them within 6–12 months of opening for ground spices and 12–18 months for whole spices. Beyond those dates, bin them and buy fresh.

Secondly Store in an airtight lidded container, in a dry place. Temperature is not important but it is better cooler rather than hotter.

Thirdly Do not be tempted to display your spices in alluring glass jars. Ultra violet and especially direct sunlight fades the colours, and more importantly the tastes. Glass is all right so long as the spices are kept in a dark place – a cupboard or pantry.

The spices you need The list on Appendix 2, page 125 will enable you to make all the dishes in this book. All of these spices are available by mail order (see page 125 for details).

Roasting spices Some recipes in this book call for roasted whole spices. Whole spices are easy and fun to roast and the results you get are stupendous. Just as when we roast coffee, the roasting process releases delicious aromatic fragrances, the essential oils, into the air.

The simplest way to roast spices is to pre-heat a dry frying pan, karahi or wok on a medium heat on the stove. When hot, add the whole spices and dry stir-fry (no oil or water, remember) for 30–60 seconds to release the aromas. Do not let the spices burn, and if you do burn them, bin them – it's cheap enough and quick enough to start again. Leave to cool and then you can store them. However it is better to roast them as required and use them immediately. Recipes in this book specify if spices should be roasted.

Grinding spices   Roast them first and cool them. Then grind in a mortar and pestle if you enjoy hard work, or in a coffee grinder or the spice mill attachment for electric food processors or liquidisers.

Garam Masala

This is the best example of roasting and grinding your own spices. Try it, at least once, please. Then compare it with any brand of factory-made garam masala. I guarantee you'll do-it-yourself from then on.

Garam means hot, and masala means mixture of spices. The heat comes from the pepper. There are as many mixtures as there are cooks, but all should use aromatic spices. Here is a particularly aromatic version, suitable for tandoori dishes. Next time you may wish to add other spices or make other changes.

Garam masala is best used towards the end of the cooking. Add it too early and you lose its aromatic qualities. It can also be sprinkled over a finished dish as a garnish. I've used metric quantities only. Tablespoons (**heaped**) are acceptable but less accurate.

~~~~~~~~~~~~~~~~~~~~~~~~~~~~

Makes 175 g (about 11 heaped tablespoons when ground)

50 g (8 tablespoons) coriander seeds

40 g (4 tablespoons) white cummin seeds

20 g (2 tablespoons) black peppercorns

20 g (several pieces) cassia bark

15 g (2 tablespoons) fennel seeds

10 g (2 tablespoons) cloves

10 g (1 tablespoon) green cardamom seeds

7 g (several) bay leaves, dried

3 g (1 teaspoon) wild onion seeds

~~~~~~~~~~~~~~~~~~~~~~~~~~~~

1   Lightly roast everything in a dry pan (see page 16). Do not let the spices burn. They should give off a light steam. When they give off an aroma, remove from the heat.

2   When cool, grind in batches.

3   After grinding the whole amount, mix thoroughly and store in an

airtight jar. It will last almost indefinitely, but for the best flavour, make in small batches every few months.

DRY GROUND SPICE MASALA MIXTURES

Many of the recipes in this book require curry or tandoori pastes. These can be purchased bottled. The Curry Club makes an excellent range based on the recipes in this book, but you may enjoy the challenge of making your own. It is not at all hard, requiring just a little of your time. To make home made bottled pastes, it is first necessary to make up a mixture of dry spices.

Mild Curry Masala (Dry Mixture)

You could use commercially blended curry powder, but here is an alternative and very aromatic do-it-yourself version.

It is better to weigh the spices, though they do vary from batch to batch in density and water content. Tablespoon measures can be used with less accuracy. This blend will mature and improve if left for a week or two before using, but it should be used within 6 months.

Makes 265 g (about 17 tablespoons when ground)

Whole spices
100 g (16 tablespoons) coriander seeds

40 g (4½ tablespoons) white cummin seed

15 g (2 tablespoons) fennel seeds

15 g (2 tablespoons) fenugreek seeds

15 g (several pieces) cassia bark

15 g (2 tablespoons) cloves

5 g (several) bay leaves

Ground spices
25 g (1¾ tablespoons) garam masala (see page 18)

25 g (1¾ tablespoons) turmeric

10 g (⅔ tablespoon) ginger

Roast and grind the whole spices then blend with the ground spices and store.

Tandoori Masala (Dry Mixture)

As with all pre-mixed masalas, this has the advantage of maturing during storage. Keep it in the dark in an airtight container, and it will be good for 6–12 months.

Makes 245 g (about 17 tablespoons)

40 g (8 teaspoons) ground coriander

35 g (7 teaspoons) ground cummin

35 g (7 teaspoons) garlic powder

35 g (7 teaspoons) paprika

25 g (5 teaspoons) ground ginger

25 g (5 teaspoons) mango powder

5 g (2 teaspoons) dried mint

25 g (5 teaspoons) beetroot powder (for deep red colouring)*

10 g (2 teaspoons) chilli powder

10 g (2 teaspoons) anatto seed powder (for yellow colouring)*

Simply mix the ingredients together well, and store. Use as described in the recipes.

FRYING GROUND SPICES

Factory ground spices are not roasted first (and that includes factory packaged garam masala). Consequently unless they are cooked first, their essential oils will not be released, and they will taste raw no matter what you do. To cook them, mix the ground spice – usually more than one spice – with an equal volume of water to make a paste. Fry that paste in oil to remove the water. The rawness is cooked out and the paste can be incorporated into subsequent cooking.

* If you use food colouring powder instead, use no more than 5 g red and 3 g sunset yellow. These small quantities will achieve a more vibrant colour than beetroot and anatto, but see page 12.

The following three recipes show how it's done.

Mild Curry Paste

This mild paste can form the base for many curry dishes. Using vinegar (rather than all water) to make the paste will enable you to preserve it in jars. As with pickling, sterilise the jars (a good hot wash in the dishwasher followed by a dry-out in a low oven will do). Top off the paste in the jar with hot oil and inspect after a few days to see that there is no mould. If there is, carefully scrape off the surface mould and re-cook the paste with some more vinegar.

~~~~~~~~~~~~~~~~~~~~~~

Makes about 1½ lb (675 g)

approx 265 g (9 oz) mild curry masala powder (1 full recipe, see page 19)

6–8 fl oz (175–250 ml) vinegar (any type)

6–8 fl oz (175–250 ml) vegetable oil

~~~~~~~~~~~~~~~~~~~~~~

1   Mix together the curry powder spices.

2   Add the vinegar and enough water to make a creamy paste.

3   Heat the oil in a karahi or wok.

4   Add the paste to the oil. It will splatter a bit so be careful.

5   Stir-fry the paste continually to prevent it sticking until the water content is cooked out (it should take 5 minutes). As the liquid is reduced, the paste will begin to make a regular bubbling noise (hard to describe, but it goes chup, chup, chup, chup) if you don't stir, and it will splatter. This is your audible cue that it is ready. You can tell if the spices are cooked by taking the karahi off the stove. Leave to stand for 3–4 minutes. If the oil 'floats' to the top, the spices are cooked. If not, add a little more oil and repeat.

6   Bottle the paste in sterilised jars. Then heat up a little more oil and 'cap' off the paste by pouring in enough oil to cover. Seal the jars and store.

Green Masala Paste

This curry paste is green in colour because of its use of coriander and mint. You can buy it factory made, but it does not have the delicious fresh taste of this recipe from Ivan Watson, journalist and regular correspondent to *The Curry Magazine*. You will come across green masala paste in the Indian home where it is used to enhance curry dishes and impart a subtle flavour that can be obtained in no other way. As with all curry pastes, this one will keep in jars indefinitely if made correctly.

Makes about 1 lb (450 g)

1 teaspoon fenugreek seeds

6 garlic cloves, chopped

2 tablespoons finely chopped fresh ginger

1½ oz (40 g) fresh mint leaves

1½ oz (40 g) fresh coriander leaves

4 fl oz (120 ml) vinegar (any type)

3 teaspoons salt

3 teaspoons turmeric

2 teaspoons chilli powder

½ teaspoon ground cloves

1 teaspoon ground cardamom seeds

4 fl oz (120 ml) vegetable oil

2 fl oz (50 ml) mustard oil (see opposite)

1 Soak the fenugreek seeds in water overnight. They will swell and acquire a jelly-like coating.

2 Next day, strain the fenugreek, discarding the water.

3 Mulch down all the ingredients, except the oils, in a blender or food processor, to make a purée.

4 Heat the two oils in a karahi or wok and cook the purée by following stages 4–6 of the mild curry paste method on page 21.

Mustard oil

Mustard seeds are a very popular Indian spice, particularly popular in the south and in Bengal. The seeds are also used to make mustard oil. It has been used for Indian cooking for thousands of years, and is available bottled at the specialist stores over here.

Recently, the manufacturers have taken to adding the phrase 'for external use only' to their label. What ever does this mean? Can it now no longer be used for cooking? Will it poison us if we eat it?

It appears that this enigmatic phrase is there as a result of European legislation. Here, from the horse's mouth – KTC Edibles Ltd in the West Midlands, a major producer of mustard oil – is the explanation: *'Pure mustard oil contains over 22% erucic acid. In large doses this can cause allergic reactions and may be carcinogenic. EC regulations stipulate that no food shall contain over 5% erucic acid, consequently KTC carry the statement 'for external use only.'*

KTC however know that this product is widely used in Asian cooking, as it has been for thousands of years. At most, one portion recipe requires a teaspoon or two, and you would need several pints a day for it to have any adverse effect. It's like the current scare about apple juice, where 1 drop of parulin, a natural toxin, per 2,000 pints is said to be above 'safety limits'. Yet you would need to drink nearly 200 pints a week to exceed the limit.

You will find an alternative to pure mustard oil in a product called blended mustard oil. Here pure mustard oil is mixed with vegetable oil, and is therefore already diluted.

Mustard oil gives a delicious and distinct flavour but if you have the slightest reservation about using it, substitute another oil (for example sesame oil) in its place.

Red Tandoori Paste

Most restaurants use bright red tandoori paste to colour and spice their marinade. It is not difficult to make your own using tandoori dry mix masala (page 20).

~~~~~~

Makes about 1½ lb (675 g)

approx 265 g (9 oz) tandoori masala dry mixture (1 full recipe, page 20)

6–8 fl oz (175–250 ml) vinegar (any type)

6–8 fl oz (175–250 ml) vegetable oil

~~~~~~

1   Mix together the tandoori masala dry mixture with the vinegar and enough water to make a creamy paste.

2   Heat the oil in a karahi or wok and cook the purée following stages 4 to 6 of the mild curry paste method on page 21.

MARINATION

The longer you marinate meat or poultry the better will be the penetration of the marinade. Storage of raw meat and poultry requires great care. If it has been once frozen then thawed, it will be acceptable to marinate in the fridge for up to 24 hours and no more. If the meat or poultry is fresh and has come straight from the vendor's fridge to your own, providing you stay within the 'use by' date, if applicable, it will be acceptable to marinate up to 60 hours in the fridge. Any marination, even after 24 hours, should be thoroughly inspected and smelt. The meat or poultry should look firm and smell clean. Longer marinations are successful using the freezer, but not if the meat or poultry has already been frozen.

Fish and shellfish can also be marinated but require much less time in the marinade than meat or poultry.

On pages 25–27 are three different tandoori marinades. To ring the changes, if you wish, you can substitute any one of them for any other in recipes in this book which call for tandoori marinades.

Red Tandoori Marinade

Yoghurt, oil, lemon juice and a little milk are used to 'suspend' the spices for this red tandoori marinade.

~~~~~~~~~~~~~~

Makes about 14 oz (400 g) marinade

5 oz (150 g) plain yoghurt

2 tablespoons vegetable oil

2 tablespoons bottled or fresh lemon juice

2 or 3 garlic cloves, chopped

2 or 3 fresh red chillies, chopped (optional)

2 tablespoons chopped fresh coriander leaves

1 teaspoon white cummin seeds, roasted and ground

1 teaspoon garam masala (page 18)

1 teaspoon mild curry paste (page 21)

2 tablespoons red tandoori paste (page 24)

1 tablespoon tomato purée

½ teaspoon salt

about 4 fl oz (100 ml) milk (maybe more, maybe less)

~~~~~~~~~~~~~~

1   Put the yoghurt, oil, lemon, garlic, chillies and fresh coriander leaves into the blender and pulse it into as fine a purée as you can get.

2   Add all the remaining ingredients except the milk and continue pulsing.

3   Now add milk until the purée is easy to pour. As there are some variables in the ingredients you may need more or less milk than stated. The colour should be creamy scarlet. Refrigerate until needed.

Note: Some recipes require about 7 oz (200 g) of marinade. Simply halve the above quantities.

Green Tandoori Marinade

Green tandoori dishes are not traditional but I've been using gorgeous herby natural colour marinades for years to achieve fine tandoori-style results.

Makes about 14 oz (400 g) marinade

5 oz (150 g) plain yoghurt

2 tablespoons vegetable oil

2 tablespoons bottled or fresh lemon juice

3–4 garlic cloves, chopped

2–3 fresh green chillies, chopped (optional)

3 tablespoons chopped fresh mint leaves

3 tablespoons chopped fresh coriander leaves

3 tablespoons green masala paste (page 22)

1 teaspoon cummin seeds, roasted and ground

1 teaspoon garam masala

½ teaspoon salt

4 fl oz approx (100 ml) milk (maybe more, maybe less)

1 Put the yoghurt, oil, lemon juice, garlic, chillies, leaves and paste into the blender and pulse it into as fine a paste as you can.

2 Add all the remaining ingredients except the milk and continue pulsing.

3 Now add enough milk to make the purée easy to pour. As there are some variables in the ingredients you may need more or less milk than stated. The colour should be creamy dark green. Refrigerate until needed.

Note: Some recipes require about 7 oz (200 g) of marinade. Simply halve the above quantities.

Raan or Aromatic Tandoori Marinade

This marinade is, perhaps, even more unusual than the previous green one. It is another of my modifications to the traditional red tandoori marinade, which concentrates on aromatics rather than colour. It was devised for *raan* (see page 38) but it works admirably for all dishes. Its colour, by the way, is neutral creamy buff, but this cooks into a gorgeous brown crispy finish.

Makes about 14 oz (400 g) marinade

5 oz (150 g) plain yoghurt

2 tablespoons sesame or mustard oil (see tip page 23)

2 tablespoons bottled or fresh lemon juice

3 or 4 garlic cloves, chopped

1 inch (2.5 cm) cube fresh ginger

2 or 3 fresh green chillies, chopped

1 tablespoon chopped fresh coriander leaves

4 tablespoons dried onion flakes

2 tablespoons ground almonds

½ teaspoon salt

4 fl oz (100 ml) milk (maybe more, maybe less)

Spices (roasted and ground)

2 tablespoons coriander seeds

1 tablespoon sesame seeds

1 teaspoon green cardamom seeds

1 teaspoon fennel seeds

1 Put the yoghurt, oil, lemon juice, garlic, ginger, chillies and leaves into the blender and pulse it into as fine a paste as you can.

2 Add all the remaining ingredients, including the spices and pulse until you get a purée which is easy to pour. You will almost certainly need a little more milk than the measured amount, but add it little by little. Refrigerate until needed.

Note: Some recipes require approximately 7 oz (200 g) of marinade. Simply halve the above quantities.

SIZZLERS

Tandoori and tikka dishes can be served to the tables very hot, smoking and sizzling like a rocket going into space. This is a restaurant technique and to do it you'll need to buy special heavy, steel sizzlers (obtainable from the Curry Club, for address see page 124). There are two types – a flat oval tray and a small two-handled karahi dish, each made of cast iron and each with a wooden base. They make an attractive presentation, but be careful not to burn yourself, your guests or your table with the excruciatingly fire-hot dishes, nor to splutter hot oil over their clothes.

Any of the dry tandoori and tikka recipes in this book can be served sizzling. The technique is simple when you know how. Here are the secrets:

1   The food is cooked to readiness in a separate pan.

2   Just prior to serving place the dry cast-iron dish directly on to the stove over a ring at its hottest. Let the steel bowl get as hot as it can. It takes at least five minutes.

3   Add a teaspoon or two of ghee or oil to the pan and turn off the heat (to prevent the oil from catching fire).

4   *Carefully* add ½ teaspoon of water or lime juice. Take care, because the hot oil and water will splutter and steam. Add the food at once. Do not load the pan over half full or you may lose the effect.

5   Take to the table, still hissing.

Remember: The pan is blisteringly hot, though still innocently black, so use oven gloves and treat it with all respect!

Tandoori Mixed Grill

One of the restaurants' most favourite presentations is the tandoori/tikka mixed grill. You can create your own mixed grill by choosing a selection of recipes from this book. Adjust quantities to suit the number of people you are serving. It's ideal for parties and barbecues – your imagination is already working overtime!

Salad Beds

Many of the tikka and tandoori dishes in this book are served on a bed of salad – but this need not be just a bed of lettuce. Here are some possibilities. Salad vegetables are not only good for you – they give a dish a fresh look with excellent colour contrasts. Buy fresh and use on the same day for best appearance.

Choose from a combination of the following and place artistically on your serving dish. Put your tikka or tandoori on the salad bed, then garnish with mustard and cress and lemon or lime wedges.

Shredded leaves   iceberg lettuce; Chinese leaf; endive top; radicchio; spinach, white cabbage etc.

Strips   red, green, yellow, orange, black or white pepper; carrot; white radish (mooli); chillies; fresh coconut

Leaves   coriander, whole, chopped or shredded, stalks removed; parsley; dill; fennel; watercress; basil

GARNISHES

Any of the above vegetables can be used to garnish curry dishes just prior to serving, improving their appearance quite considerably. The following items can also be used:

Nuts   such as pistachio, almonds and cashew can be added whole or chopped, raw 'roasted' or fried. Do not use salted nuts.

Onions   dried fried onion flakes are attractive and crunchy and can easily be bought ready to use.

Leafy herbs   can be used raw but for a fascinating change try deep-frying them (375°F/190°C). It only takes a few seconds. They whoosh and go dark green almost at once. Remove from the oil and rest on kitchen paper. They will go crispy quite soon. Then serve.

Cream   a curl of cream can look attractive.

CHAPTER 2

Meat

There is no question about it, tandoori cooking was devised for meat. The long marination not only gave flavour to the meat, it tenderised it. Meat, in India, to this day is much tougher and leaner than its Western counterpart, the animals leading a much harder life, without benefit of overfeeding.

Traditionally, the meat used was mutton, goat or for special occasions lamb or kid. We can extend the range by using beef, veal, pork or venison.

Use the best cuts you can afford. This generally comes from the rump or rear leg. It is the leanest and most tender. Lesser priced cuts contain more unwanted matter, such as gristle, sinews etc, and are generally more fatty. Remember that as the fat melts during cooking, the piece of meat will shrink, so buying cheap is often a false economy.

Meat Tikka

Best quality meat gives best results. When cooked it should be tender, yet slightly chewy, like a good steak. Use any lean filleted meat – beef, pork, venison or veal. The traditional meat is lamb.

Serves 2 as a starter

7 oz (200 g) red tandoori marinade (page 25)

8–10 chunky pieces lean meat cut into 1½ inch (3.75 cm) cubes

1   Mix the marinade ingredients in a large non-metallic bowl.

2   Place the cubes of meat into the marinade, ensuring they are well coated. Cover the bowl and refrigerate for 24 hours minimum, 60 hours maximum (see page 24).

3   When ready to cook, preheat oven to 425°F/220°C/Gas 7. Line an oven tray with foil and place the oven rack above the tray.

4   Remove the meat from the marinade and thread the cubes on to two skewers, leaving a little space between each chunk (this helps heat transference).

5   Place the skewers on to an oven rack, and cook for 15–20 minutes, depending on your oven. A degree of pinkness or rareness in the middle of the meat may be preferred, and this is acceptable – except for pork which should be fully cooked – adjust cooking times accordingly. Serve on a bed of salad with lemon wedges and tandoori chutney.

Shashlik Kebab

You'll find the shashlik kebab at a number of Indian restaurants. The principle is to thread marinated meat (or chicken or seafood) on to skewers interspersed with onion, and red or green pepper. The method is straightforward, and has probably been around as long as cooking itself. What could be easier than to pick up a piece of meat on the tip of a sword and grill it over a fire? Here I use bamboo skewers, which should be soaked in water for 1 hour before use, to make them more resistant to burning.

~~~~~~~~~~~~~~~~~~~~~~~~~~~~~~~

Serves 2 as a starter

8 oz (225 g) topside of beef or fillet or sirloin steak 1 inch (2.5 cm) thick

½ red pepper

½ green pepper

½ Spanish onion

2 cloves garlic, peeled (optional)

2 green chillies (optional)

Marinade
4 tablespoons olive or soy oil

1 teaspoon ground cummin

½ teaspoon powdered cassia bark or cinnamon

6 tablespoons red wine

1 tablespoon lemon juice

2 teaspoons tomato purée

½ teaspoon puréed or finely chopped garlic

~~~~~~~~~~~~~~~~~~~~~~~~~~~~~~~

1   Thoroughly mix together all the marinade ingredients in a large non-metallic bowl.

2   Discard any gristle, fat etc from the meat and cut into ten cubes (minimum size of 1 inch/2.5 cm each). Use any off-cuts for another recipe or stock.

3   Add the meat to the marinade, mix well then cover with cling film and leave to stand in the fridge for a minimum of 24 hours, a maximum of 60 (see page 24).

4   After the meat has marinated, cut the red pepper into four 1 inch (2.5 cm) diamonds or squares. Do the same with the green pepper. Separate the layers of the onion and cut ten pieces into the same sized diamonds or squares. (Use leftover pepper and onion for a cachumber salad, page 122.)

5   Pre-heat the oven to 425°F/220°C/Gas 7. Meanwhile thread the items on to two skewers as follows: onion, meat, green pepper, meat, onion, red pepper, meat, onion, green pepper, meat, onion, red pepper, meat, onion. Put a clove of garlic and/or one green chilli on to each skewer (optional). Ensure all items are close together but not squashed.

6   Place the skewers on to a wire rack and the rack on to an oven tray or drip pan. Baste the skewers with the excess marinade.

7   Cook for 8–10 minutes for rare meat, 10–15 for medium, and 15 and more for well done. Alternatively cook for the same amount of time under a medium grill with the rack at the lowest level. Or cook over the barbecue.

Hassina Kebab

The shashlik kebab (previous recipe) made its way eastwards in ancient times from the Middle East to Iran where, with modifications to the spicing but the same style of cooking, it became known as the hasina kebab. You'll find it in India, and at the Indian restaurant where it is also called the hussaini kebab.

    This version uses meat tikka pieces, threaded with onion and pieces of green and red pepper.

Serves 2 as a starter

7 oz (200 g) red tandoori marinade (page 25)

10 chunky pieces lean meat, cut into 1 inch (2.5 cm cubes)

½ red pepper

½ green pepper

½ Spanish onion

2 cloves garlic, peeled (optional)

2 green chillies (optional)

1   Mix the marinade ingredients in a large non-metallic bowl.

2   Add the cubes of meat to the marinade, ensuring that they are well coated. Cover the bowl with cling film and refrigerate for 24 hours minimum, 60 hours maximum (see page 24).

3   After the meat has marinated, cut the red pepper into four 1 inch (2.5 cm) diamonds or squares. Do the same with the green pepper. Separate the layers of the onion and cut ten pieces into the same sized diamonds or squares. (Use leftover pepper and onion for a cachumber salad, page 122.)

4   Pre-heat the oven to 425°F/220°C/Gas 7 and meanwhile thread the items on to two skewers as follows: onion, meat, green pepper, meat, onion, red pepper, meat, onion, green pepper, meat, onion, red pepper, meat, onion. Put a clove of garlic and/or one green chilli on to each skewer (optional). Ensure all items are close together but not squashed.

5   Place the skewers on a wire rack and the rack on an oven tray. Baste the skewers with the excess marinade.

6   Cook for 8–10 minutes for rare meat, 10–15 for medium, and 15 and more for well done. Alternatively, cook under a medium grill with the rack at the lowest level for the same amounts of time. Or cook over the barbecue.

Tandoori Steak

Steaks are not traditional tandoori ingredients. This is because Indian food is not traditionally eaten with cutlery. I think tandoori steaks are a great idea – and you can use any meat, not just beef. Try also lamb or pork steaks. They are cooked on the grill here, but could also be barbecued.

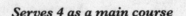

Serves 4 as a main course

4 steaks each weighing 6–8 oz (175–225 g)

14 oz (400 g) red, green or raan tandoori marinade (pages 25–27)

1   Prick the steaks all over with a fork and coat thoroughly with the marinade in a non-metallic bowl.

2 Cover with cling film and put in the fridge for a minimum of 24 hours, maximum 60 hours (see page 24).

3 To cook, preheat the grill to high heat.

4 Put the steaks on a rack above a foil-lined grill tray and place this in the midway position under the heat. For rare steaks, cook for about 4 minutes, turning at least once. Cook longer if you prefer your meat better done. Pork must be thoroughly cooked, but beef or lamb can be served rare.

5 To finish off, raise the tray nearer to the heat and singe the steaks to obtain a little blackening. Serve on a bed of salad with lemon wedges, naan bread and tandoori chutney.

Tandoori Lamb Chop

Chops are a less than traditional tandoori ingredient. The reason seems to be that meat with bone is preferred wet cooked (i.e. in a curry) to get the most out of the bones. (Indians love to suck bones in curry.) Of course they ideally suit the tandoori process – *and* you can suck them to your heart's content!

Serves 2 as part of the main course, 4 as a starter

8 lamb chops, about 4 oz (115 g) each

14 oz (400 g) red tandoori marinade (page 25)

1 Remove some but not all of the fat from the chops and prick the meat all over with a fork. Coat the chops in the marinade in a non-metallic bowl.

2 Cover with cling film and put into the fridge for a minimum of 24 hours, maximum 60 hours (see page 24).

3 To cook, preheat the grill to high heat.

4 Put the chops on a foil-lined grill tray and place this in the midway position under the heat. Alternatively they can be barbecued.

5   Cook for about 8 minutes, turn over and cook for a further 8 minutes or so. Serve on a bed of salad with lemon wedges, naan bread and tandoori chutney.

Tikka Ribs

You would never find pork in Afghanistan or Pakistan, both fervent Moslem countries to whom pork is forbidden. Serve these finger-licking ribs as part of a tandoori mixed grill (see page 28). Ensure the meat is thoroughly cooked before serving.

~~~~~~~~~~~~~~~~~~~

Serves 2 as part of a main course or 4 as a starter

16 tiny barbecue pork ribs, each weighing 1 oz (25 g), or 12 larger ones

7 oz (200 g) red tandoori marinade (page 25)

~~~~~~~~~~~~~~~~~~~

1   Prick the meat with a fork and coat the ribs in the marinade in a non-metallic bowl.

2   Cover with cling film and put into the fridge for a minimum of 24, maximum 60 hours (see page 24).

3   To cook, preheat the grill to high heat.

4   Put the ribs on a rack above a foil lined grill tray and place this in the midway position under the heat. Alternatively they can be barbecued.

5   Cook for about 5 minutes for tiny ribs, a bit longer for larger ribs. Turn and cook for a further few minutes. Serve on a bed of salad with lemon wedges, naan bread and tandoori chutney.

Sheek Kebabs

There are two fundamentally different methods to make sheek kebabs. One is to boil the mince then blend it with lentils and bind it with egg and flour. It gives a creamy silky result and is called the reshmi kebab, but it takes an age to make. The method given below is much quicker. The meat is 'chewier' but equally delicious.

You can use cheaper cuts of meat, but you won't get better kebabs than with fillet steak.

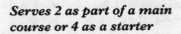

Serves 2 as part of a main course or 4 as a starter

1½ lb (675 g) fillet steak, weighed after discarding fat and unwanted matter

1 tablespoon dried onion flakes

2 garlic cloves, finely chopped

0 to 4 fresh green chillies, chopped

1 tablespoon red tandoori paste (page 24)

1 tablespoon garam masala

1 tablespoon chopped fresh mint

1 tablespoon chopped fresh coriander

1 teaspoon salt

1 Chop the meat into strips.

2 Run it through a hand or electric mincer two or three times until it is lump free and finely ground.

3 In a large bowl mix all the ingredients together by hand. The mixture should be fairly sticky. Clean your hands.

4 Divide the mixture into four. Make into four sausage shapes and slip these on to metal skewers.

5 To cook, preheat the grill to high heat.

6 Put the skewers on to a rack above a foil-lined grill tray and place this in the midway position under the heat. Alternatively, they can be barbecued. Cook for about 8 to 10 minutes, turning at least once.

7 To finish off raise the tray nearer to the heat and singe the kebabs to obtain a little blackening. Serve on a bed of salad with lemon wedges, naan bread and tandoori chutney.

Tandoori Hare (or rabbit)

Not encountered in the average tandoori house, perhaps, but an excellent subject for this style of cooking, being the ideal size and of good flavour. One 5 lb (2.25 kg) skinned hare or rabbit will yield about 1¼ lb (560 g) meat. Keep it on the bone, but get it jointed into legs and back pieces.

Serves 4 as a starter

6 or 8 hare or rabbit pieces, skinned and on the bone

14 oz (400 g) red tandoori marinade (page 25)

1   Prick the meat with a fork and coat thoroughly with the marinade in a non-metallic bowl.

2   Cover with cling film and put in the fridge for a minimum of 24 hours, maximum of 60 hours (see page 24).

3   To cook, preheat the grill to medium heat.

4   Put the meat on to a rack above a foil-lined grill tray and place this in the midway position under the heat. Alternatively, they can be barbecued.

5   Cook for 15–20 minutes, turning at least once. Test that the pieces are cooked to your liking. To finish off, raise the tray nearer to the heat and singe the meat pieces to obtain a little blackening. Serve on a bed of salad with lemon wedges, naan bread and tandoori chutney.

Raan (Indian Roast Leg of Lamb)

This is a traditional Indian dish devised centuries ago for the Moghul emperors and cooked in the clay oven. Cook it in the conventional oven very slowly until it is so tender, the flesh just falls off the bone.

~~~~~~~~~~~~~~~~~~~~~~~

*Serves 4 as part of a main
course*

3½ lb–4 lb (1.5–1.8 kg) leg
of lamb on the bone

14 oz (400 g) raan tandoori
marinade (page 27)

Garnish
20–30 whole raw almonds,
fried

20–30 whole fresh coriander
leaves

~~~~~~~~~~~~~~~~~~~~~~~

1 Pare away all the fat and skin membrane from the meat. Stab it all over with a small knife and coat thoroughly with the marinade in a non-metallic bowl.

2 Cover with cling film and put in the fridge for a minimum of 24 hours, a maximum of 60 hours (see page 24).

3 To cook, preheat the oven to 350°F/180°C/Gas 4 maximum. Transfer the lamb and marinade to a roasting dish and slow-roast for about 3 hours. When really tender, the flesh should literally fall off the bone.

4 Prior to serving, let it rest for 30 minutes or so in a low oven.

5 Garnish by covering with fried almonds, then sprinkle with fresh coriander leaves, the gravy from the roasting pan and any sediment from the bottom of the pan. Accompany with roast tikka potatoes (see page 71) and a vegetable dish from Chapter Five.

Tandoori Roast Topside of Beef

A gorgeous modern variation of the previous classic, which makes a marvellous change for Sunday lunch.

~~~~~~~~~~~~~~~~~~~~~~~

Serves 4 to 6

2½–3½ lb (1.1–1.5 kg) piece of beef topside,
weighed after removing all fat and membrane

14 oz (400 g) red tandoori marinade (see page 25)

~~~~~~~~~~~~~~~~~~~~~~~

1   Pare away all fat and skin membrane from the meat. Stab it all over with a small knife and coat thoroughly with the marinade in a non-metallic bowl.

2   Cover with cling film and put in the fridge for a minimum of 24 hours, a maximum of 60 hours (see page 24).

3   To cook, preheat the oven to 350°F/180°C/Gas 4 maximum. Transfer the meat to a roasting dish and slow roast for about 2 hours, until really tender.

4   Prior to serving, let it rest for 30 minutes or so in a low oven. Serve with roast tikka potatoes (see page 71) and a vegetable dish from Chapter Five.

Tandoori Turban Crown Roast of Lamb

Here's an invention of mine, or rather a modification of an old classic favourite. The meat is the ribs from the 'best end neck' of the lamb. Your butcher will remove unwanted matter and form the crown using at least 14 cutlet ribs, on top of which will be placed 'cutlet frills', which from now on we'll call 'turbans'. Ask for the crown plain, 'without cap and filling', (some butchers fill the crown with fat taken from the ribs, but you don't want this). Ask for spare turbans, just in case!

Serves 4

One 14–16 rib crown roast

14 oz (400 g) **raan tandoori marinade (page 27)**

Stuffing
8 oz (225 g) **cooked boiled rice, cold**

4 oz (110 g) **fresh spinach, shredded**

2 tablespoons **dried onion flakes**

1 tablespoon **green masala paste (page 22)**

1 Remove and keep the 'turbans'. Weigh the crown before you start and make a note of it. Prick the cutlets with a fork and coat thoroughly with the marinade in a non-metallic bowl.

2 Cover with cling film and put in the fridge for a minimum of 24 hours, a maximum of 60 hours (see page 24).

3 To cook, preheat the oven to 350°F/180°C/Gas 4. Mix the stuffing ingredients together.

4 Carefully put the crown on to an oven tray, then pack the stuffing into the centre and spoon the excess marinade on top of the stuffing. Cap the stuffing with a shaped piece of foil and put the tray into the oven. Calculate cooking time from your noted weight, roasting for 25 minutes per pound (450 g) plus 20 minutes. Baste at least twice during cooking with juices from the oven pan.

5 To serve, place the roast on to a warm serving dish. There should be some liquid in the oven tray. Discard excess oil and pour the juices into the stuffing. Replace the turbans and serve with naan bread, vegetables and roast tikka potatoes (see page 71).

Liver Tikka

I find grilling liver can dry it up too much. Here it is very simply cooked as a stir-fry. Heart, brain or kidney can be substituted for liver or a combination can be used. Prior to using, chop up your offal to the size required by the recipe then soak it in milk for a couple of hours or more. This leaches out some of the bitterness and greatly improves the flavour. Drain and dry the offal before using. Discard the milk.

Serves 4 as a starter

1 lb (450 g) lamb's liver, chopped into 1 inch (2.5 cm) cubes

7 oz (200 g) red tandoori marinade (page 25)

4 tablespoons ghee or vegetable oil

1 teaspoon cummin seeds

salt to taste

1   In a non-metallic bowl, mix the liver with the marinade. Cover and refrigerate for 6–24 hours.

2   To cook, heat the ghee or oil in a large karahi or wok. Add the cummin seeds, then the liver pieces, shaking off any excess marinade. Stir-fry for 5–8 minutes.

3   Test that the liver is cooked by cutting through a piece. It should not be rare. Salt to taste. Serve on a bed of salad with naan bread and lemon wedges.

Tandoori Spiced Sausage

This remarkable recipe works with any type of sausage, requiring just the oven to achieve great results. Serve with tandoori baked potatoes (see page 70) or chips.

Serves 2 for a main course, 4 as a starter

8 sausages (around 1 lb/450 g)

7 oz (200 g) red tandoori marinade (page 25)

1–2 teaspoons English mustard

1 tablespoon ghee or vegetable oil

---

1   Mix the marinade and mustard in a large non-metallic bowl. Add the sausages, ensuring they are well coated.

2   Cover with cling film and put in the fridge for a minimum of 24 hours, a maximum of 60 hours (page 24).

3   To cook, preheat the oven to 375°F/190°C/Gas 5.

4   Spread the ghee or oil over a warmed oven tray and place the sausages on it, so that they don't touch each other.

5   Cook for 20 minutes, then turn and baste the sausages using any excess marinade. Cook for a further 20–25 minutes.

6   Serve at once piping hot. Alternatively they are superb cold, particularly as a sandwich filler.

Note What could be better for the barbecue? It is best to par-cook them for 20–30 minutes in the oven and then finish off on the barbecue.

Sweetbread Tikka

There are two types of sweetbread. One type is the thymus gland, found in the throats of piglets, calves and lambs. The other is the pancreas (near the stomach), which is larger than the former. Calves' sweetbreads are preferred, being 'milder'. Their spongy texture is an acquired taste and they need preparation before you can use them, but tikka-style cooking suits sweetbreads really well.

~~~~~~~~~~~~~~~~~~~~~~~~~~~~~~~~~

Serves 2 as a starter

1 lb (450 g) calves' sweetbreads

7 oz (200 g) red tandoori marinade (page 25)

~~~~~~~~~~~~~~~~~~~~~~~~~~~~~~~~~

1 Soak the sweetbreads in cold water for 5–6 hours until they turn white. Rinse them and change the water several times during this period.

2 Give them a final rinse then put them in a saucepan and cover with salted cold water. Bring to the boil. Drain immediately and rinse the sweetbreads under the cold tap.

3 Remove the unwanted matter – skin, gristle and fibres etc, from the sweetbreads, then cut into suitable pieces for skewering. As they will be irregular in size and shape, it is not possible to say how many pieces you will get.

4 Place the sweetbread pieces and the marinade into a non-metallic bowl. Mix well to coat.

5 Cover with cling film and refrigerate for a minimum of 24 hours and a maximum of 60 hours (see page 24).

6 Just prior to cooking, divide the sweetbread pieces between two skewers. (Use spare marinade in a curry or discard.)

7   Preheat the grill to medium.

8   Place the skewers on an oven rack above a foil-lined oven tray and place this in the midway position under the grill. Alternatively they can be barbecued.

9   Cook for 4 minutes, turn and cook for a further 4 minutes. Cut through one piece to check that it is cooked – it should be white right through. If not, cook for a few more minutes.

10   To finish off, raise the tray nearer to the heat and singe the pieces to obtain a little blackening. Serve on a bed of salad with lemon wedges, naan bread and tandoori chutney.

Jeerey Meerey Wild Boar

The Goan marinade used in this recipe was inspired by chef Cyrus Todiwalla of Namaste restaurant, London E1. It is comprised largely of *jeera* (cummin) and *mirchi* (black pepper). Little black hairy pigs, not unlike wild boar, are herded in Goa and their meat is deliciously gamey. Wild boar, available from game butchers in this country, has a superb gamey flavour and is much redder than pork. Wensleydale Wild Boar from the Lake District goes particularly well with this spicing. They are free-ranged in North Yorkshire and grow to around 90 lb (40.5 g) in weight. Various cuts are available by mail order from Anthony Hill, Wensleydale Wild Boar Breeders, Manor Farm, Thornton Steward, Ripon, North Yorkshire. Telephone 01677 60239.

~~~~~~~~~~~~~

Serves 2 as a starter

8–10 chunky pieces lean wild boar cut from the leg into 1½ inch (4 cm) cubes

Marinade

5 oz (150 g) plain yoghurt

2 tablespoons walnut oil

2 tablespoons lime juice

3 or 4 garlic cloves, chopped

2 or 3 fresh green chillies, chopped

4 tablespoons dried onion flakes

½ teaspoon salt

about 4 fl oz (100 ml) milk

Spices (roasted and ground)

4 tablespoons white cummin seeds

1 tablespoon black peppercorns

~~~~~~~~~~~~~~~~~~~~

1   First make the marinade. Put the yoghurt, oil, lime juice, garlic, chillies, onion and salt into the blender and pulse it into as fine a paste as you can.

2   Add the milk, and cummin seeds and black peppercorns and pulse until you get a purée which is easy to pour. You will almost certainly need a little more milk than the measured amount, but add it little by little.

3   Transfer the marinade to a large non-metallic bowl. Add the cubes of meat, ensuring they are well coated.

4   Cover the bowl with cling film and refrigerate for a minimum of 24 hours and a maximum of 60 hours (see page 24).

5   To cook, preheat the oven to 425°F/220°C/Gas 7.

6   Line an oven tray with foil and place the oven rack above the tray.

7   Remove the meat from the marinade and thread the cubes on to skewers, leaving a little space between chunks (this helps heat transference).

8   Place the skewers on the oven rack and cook for 15–20 minutes, depending on your oven. Wild boar must be fully cooked and cannot be served rare. When it is cooked serve on a bed of salad with lemon wedges and tandoori chutney.

CHAPTER 3

Poultry

The domestic chicken is said to be related to and descended from the Indian jungle fowl *Gallus Gallus*. It has been farmed for thousands of years in the ancient civilisations, such as that of Egypt. Evidence from the excavations of India's first civilisation at the Indus Valley have revealed surprisingly few charred chicken bones, compared with meat bones, indicating that chicken was rarely on the menu.

Even to this day, chicken is still regarded as a luxury item in the original Tandoori area of Pakistan. This is far from the case in the developed countries, where chicken is prolific and relatively inexpensive. Because of this, and the fact that dietitians promote chicken as being relatively cholesterol free, chicken has become more popular than red meat.

More than that, chicken tikka and chicken tikka masala have become the most popular starter and main dish curry at the tandoori house. These plus a number of other interesting chicken and poultry recipes appear in this chapter.

Tandoori Whole Chicken

For best results try to obtain a farm-fresh double poussin (a 6–10 week old young chicken) whose 'oven-ready' weight is 1½–2 lb (675–900 g).

~~~~~~~~~~~~~~~~~~~~

Serves 2–4 as a starter

1 double poussin (see above)

juice of 2 lemons

7 oz (200 g) red tandoori marinade (page 25)

~~~~~~~~~~~~~~~~~~~~

1 Remove and discard the skin, and clean the chicken inside and out. With the tip of a sharp knife, make short gashes all over the flesh (this gives a greater surface area for the marinade). Rub all over with the lemon juice (this degreases it and makes the marinade penetrate better). Leave to dry for about 30 minutes.

2 Put the chicken into a large non-metallic bowl. Cover with the marinade, massaging it into the gashes. Cover the bowl and refrigerate for 24 hours–60 hours (see page 24).

3 To cook, preheat the oven to 375°F/190°C/Gas 5. Place the chicken on a skewer lengthwise, and place at the top of the oven. Put a tray lined with foil underneath to catch the drips.

4 Cook for 20 minutes, then turn over. Continue to cook for 20–30 more minutes, until cooked through. To check, prick the leg. If clear liquid runs out (rather than red), it is cooked. Serve with salad, onion rings and lemon wedges, naan bread and tandoori chutney.

Tandoori Whole Duck

This is a variation of the previous recipe. Use a duckling of about 3½ lb (1.5 kg) for two people as it yields less meat than chicken. You can use a different flavoured marinade if you wish.

While cooking, the marinade caramelises into a fantastic crispy coating. Delicious!

~~~~~~~~~~~~~~~~~~~~~~~~~~

Serves 2 as a starter

3½ lb (1.5 kg) duckling

juice of 2 lemons

14 oz (400 g) raan tandoori marinade (page 27)

~~~~~~~~~~~~~~~~~~~~~~~~~~

1 Remove and discard the skin and clean the duckling inside and out. Poke a sharp knife deep into the duck all over, then rub with lemon juice. Leave to dry for 30 minutes in a deep bowl. Discard any spare lemon juice.

2 Now work the marinade into the duck. Cover the bowl and refrigerate for 24 to 60 hours (see page 24).

3 To cook, preheat the oven to 350°F/180°C/Gas 4. Meanwhile, remove the duck from the bowl, shaking off any excess marinade, and place on an oven tray. Smear some of the excess marinade back on to the duck – enough to give it an even coating.

4 Put the duck into the oven. The total roasting time will be about 1½ hours (allowing 30 minutes per lb/450 g). After about 45 minutes, remove the duck and baste it with the remaining marinade. Return to the oven, and after a further ½ hour pierce the plump part of the leg. If it is cooked, the fluid that runs out will be clear; if not cook for longer.

5 When cooked, place the duck in a low oven to rest for 15 minutes, then cut into two servings (i.e. a half duck per person).

Tandoori Stuffed and Glazed Quail

Any small game bird can be tandoori cooked with excellent results. This version uses quail but you can use snipe or squab (young pigeon) or the larger grouse, woodcock or partridge. The glaze makes it quite outstandingly tasty.

~~~~~~~~~~~~~~~~~~~~~~~

Serves 2

2 quail, skinned

7 oz (200 g) red tandoori marinade (see page 25)

4 oz (110 g) cooked plain rice

3 tablespoons clear honey

1 tablespoon Worcester sauce

~~~~~~~~~~~~~~~~~~~~~~~

1 Clean the quails inside and out, then place in a non-metallic bowl.

2 Add the marinade, mix well then cover and put in the fridge for 24 to 60 hours (see page 24).

3 To cook, pre-heat the oven to 375°F/190°C/Gas 5.

4 Remove the quails from the marinade and mix a tablespoon or so of it with the rice. Cram the quails full of the rice to stuff them. Put them on to a foil-lined oven tray and spoon any surplus marinade over them. Roast for 10 minutes.

5 Heat the honey and Worcester sauce in a small pan to make the glaze. Cover the quails with the glaze and roast for a further 5–8 minutes. Serve on a bed of salad with lime wedges.

Note Boned quail are even better for this recipe. You can order them boned or do it yourself if you are prepared for a fiddly job. Keep the skin on.

Tandoori Bhare Murgh

This is a whole Stuffed and Roasted Chicken, also known as *Kurzi*. The result should be crispy and dry, and spicy and mouth-watering. Serve with roast tikka potatoes (page 71).

~~~~~~~~~~~~~~~~~~~~~~~~~~~~~~

Serves 4 as a main course

3½–3¾ lb (1.5–1.75 kg) roasting chicken

juice of 3 lemons

14 oz (400 g) red tandoori marinade (page 25)

6 tablespoons ghee or vegetable oil

4 garlic cloves, finely chopped

salt

2 tablespoons chopped, fresh coriander

Stuffing
8 oz (225 g) cooked Basmati rice

4 oz (110 g) frozen mixed vegetables, thawed

4 fl oz (100 ml) Greek yoghurt

¼ teaspoon salt

Spices
1 teaspoon white cummin seeds

1 teaspoon coriander seeds

½ teaspoon black peppercorns

½ teaspoon black cummin seeds

½ teaspoon turmeric

~~~~~~~~~~~~~~~~~~~~~~~~~~~~~~

1 Skin the chicken and clean it inside and out. Gash the flesh with the tip of a sharp knife and rub with the lemon juice to de-grease it. Leave to dry for 30 minutes.

2 Put the chicken in a large non-metallic bowl and work the marinade well into the chicken. Cover and refrigerate for 24 to 60 hours (see page 24).

3 Heat the ghee or oil in a large karahi or wok. Carefully place the chicken in and fry until all sides are browned (about 15 minutes). Remove from the pan, leaving the ghee and any cooked marinade behind.

4 Mix together the stuffing ingredients. When the chicken is cold enough, stuff with the mixture.

5 Fry the garlic in the ghee left in the pan, add the spices and salt to taste, and simmer gently. Add ¼ pint (150 ml) water bit by bit

over 10 minutes. Meanwhile heat the oven to 400°F/200°C/
Gas 6.

6   Put the chicken on its back in a large lidded casserole dish and
pour the fried blend over it. Put the lid on and place into the
preheated oven. Cook for about an hour, basting once or twice.

7   Remove the lid and sprinkle the fresh coriander over the chicken.
Cook without the lid for at least another 10 minutes. You'll probably need longer, and possibly an increase in heat to crust and
dry the chicken – it's up to you, but keep a close eye on it.

8   Strain off any spare oil (keep for future use) and serve with rice.

Chicken Tikka with Keema

This fine recipe, which some restaurants call *Rezela*, can be likened
to Chicken Kiev. A fillet of chicken breast is slit to make a pocket
and is then stuffed with spiced raw mince (kebab mixture) and
baked or barbecued.

~~~~~~~~~~~~~~~~

Serves 4 as a starter

**4 × 6 oz (175 g) chicken
breasts, weighed after
skinning and boning**

**14 oz (400 g) red tandoori
marinade (page 25)**

**8 oz (225 g) sheek kebab
mixture (page 36, prepared
to end of stage 3)**

salad garnish

lemon wedges

chutney

~~~~~~~~~~~~~~~~

1   Carefully cut a pocket into each chicken breast.

2   Make the marinade in a large non-metallic bowl, then cover the
breasts completely with it. Cover the bowl and refrigerate for 24
hours to 60 hours (see page 24).

3   When ready to cook, preheat the oven to its hottest. Line an oven
tray with foil and place an oven rack above the tray.

4   Press the kebab mixture into the pockets of each breast.

5   Put the breasts on the rack and cook for 14–18 minutes.

6   When cooked completely, serve on a bed of salad with lemon wedges and chutney.

Chicken Tikka Pieces

One of the most popular and delicious dishes ever. It is now of world-class status. For the equally popular chicken tikka masala, see page 84.

~~~~~~~~~~~~~~~~~~~~~~

Serves 2 as a starter

12 oz (375 g) chicken breast, skinned, filleted and cut into about 10 1½ inch (3.75 cm) cubes

7 oz (200 g) red tandoori marinade (page 25)

~~~~~~~~~~~~~~~~~~~~~~

1   Place the chicken and marinade into a non-metallic bowl. Cover and refrigerate for 24 hours to 60 hours (see page 24).

2   Just prior to cooking divide the meat between two skewers. (Use spare marinade in a curry or discard.)

3   Preheat the grill to medium. Place the skewers on an oven rack above a foil-lined grill tray and place this in the midway position. Alternatively they can be barbecued.

4   Cook for 5 minutes, turn, then cook for a further 5 minutes.

5   Cut through one piece to ensure that it is fully cooked – it should be white right through with no hint of pink. If not, cook for a while longer. When fully cooked, raise the tray nearer to the heat and singe the pieces to obtain a little blackening. Serve on a bed of salad with lemon wedges, naan bread and tandoori chutney.

Green Tandoori Chicken Tikka

This is an exciting variation of the previous (red) chicken tikka recipe, using a gorgeous herby green marinade instead.

~~~~~~~~~~~~~~~~

Serves 2 as a starter

12 oz (375 g) chicken breast, fillet skinned, and cut into 8–10 1½ inch (3.75 cm) cubes

7 oz (200 g) green tandoori marinade (page 26)

~~~~~~~~~~~~~~~~

Follow exactly the method of the previous recipe.

Duck Tikka Pieces

Duck breast makes excellent tikka. In this variation of the previous two recipes, we use raan marinade. You can, of course, use the red or green marinades instead.

~~~~~~~~~~~~~~~~

Serves 2 as a starter

12 oz (375 g) of duck breast fillet, skinned, and cut into 8–10 1½ inch (3.75 cm) cubes

7 oz (200 g) raan tandoori marinade (page 27)

~~~~~~~~~~~~~~~~

Follow exactly the method of the chicken tikka recipe opposite.

Tandoori Duck Breast

Obtain top-quality filleted duck breasts. Magret de Canard are best. They will be supplied with a fatty layer of skin which must be removed before marinating.

~~~~~~~~~~~~~~~~

Serves 2 as a main course

2 skinless duck breasts, each weighing 6–8 oz (175–225 g) after the fat is removed

7 oz (200 g) red tandoori marinade (page 25)

1 Slash the duck breasts with a knife, place in a non-metallic bowl and coat thoroughly with the marinade.

2 Cover and refrigerate for 24 to 60 hours (see page 24).

3 To cook, preheat the grill to high heat. Put the breasts on to a rack above a foil-lined grill tray and place this in the midway position under the heat. Alternatively, they can be barbecued.

4 Cook for 6–8 minutes, turning at least once.

5 To finish off, raise the tray nearer to the heat to obtain a little blackening. Serve on a bed of salad with lemon wedges, naan bread and tandoori chutney.

Tandoori Chicken Legs

Use the entire leg – the 'drumstick' (the joint below the knee and above the ankle) and the thigh.

Serves 2

2 chicken legs (see above)

juice of 1 lemon

7 oz (200 g) red tandoori marinade (page 25)

1 Skin the chicken legs, keeping each in one piece. Gash the flesh with the tip of a knife and rub in the lemon juice. Allow to dry.

2 Mix the marinade and legs in a large non-metallic bowl. Cover and refrigerate for 24–60 hours (see page 24).

3 To cook, preheat the grill to medium heat.

4   Put the legs on to a rack above a foil-lined grill tray and place this in the midway position under the heat. Alternatively, they can be barbecued.

5   Cook for at least 10 minutes, turning at least once. Depending on their size and weight they will almost certainly need longer. Test by piercing the plumpest part of the leg. The fluid which runs out must be clear and not red. If not clear, cook for longer.

6   To finish off, raise the tray nearer to the heat and singe the legs to obtain a little blackening. Serve on a bed of salad with lemon wedges, naan bread and tandoori chutney.

Tandoori Chicken Joints

Other joints of chicken can be cooked this way. Remove the skin first, then follow the above recipe. Adjust the cooking time according to the thickness and size of the joints.

Stuffed Tandoori Turkey

Turkey meat comes in quite sizeable pieces, and it is easy to fillet and stuff the breast or leg. This combination of spicy ground kebab beef inserted into tandoori marinated turkey is a winner.

Serves 2 as part of a main course

2 × 6 oz (175 g) pieces of turkey breast or thigh, skinned and filleted

4 oz (110 g) uncooked sheek kebab mix (page 36)

7 oz (200 g) raan tandoori marinade (page 27)

1   Carefully cut a pocket in each turkey piece. Insert half the kebab mixture into each slit. Put the two pieces into a non-metallic bowl and coat thoroughly with the marinade.

2   Cover and refrigerate for 24–60 hours (see page 24).

3 To cook, preheat the grill to high heat. Put the pieces on a rack above a foil-lined grill tray and place this in the midway position. Alternatively, they can be barbecued.

4 Cook for 15–20 minutes, turning at least once.

5 To finish off, raise the tray nearer to the heat and singe the turkey pieces to obtain a little blackening. Cut the pieces cross-wise into 6 or 7 slices each and serve with rice and a vegetable dish.

CHAPTER 4

Fish and Shellfish

Until relatively recently the people of Britain relied quite heavily on fish in their diet. Coastal fishermen and freshwater anglers had a much larger role to play than they do today, as did the traditional fishmonger.

Today, it is supermarkets rather than fishmongers who buy and sell the most fish and shellfish, and they offer an ever increasing range of fresh chilled produce.

If you are not a big fish-eater, it is worth spending a little time studying the fish counter, whether at a supermarket or your local fishmonger. Don't be afraid to ask for advice when choosing what to buy, and if the thought of preparing fish puts you off, get it done at the counter.

Though not traditionally found in the authentic tandoori cooking of the ancients, fish and shellfish adapt very well to the process and make a delightful alternative. Marination times are much shorter than those of meat and poultry.

Tandoori Skate

Skate is a very meaty fish and one large wing will easily serve four people as a starter.

~~~~~~~~~~~~~~~~~~~~~~

Serves 4 as a starter

1½–2 lb (700–900 g) wing of skate

juice of 2 lemons

1 teaspoon salt

½ teaspoon turmeric

7 oz (200 g) red tandoori marinade (page 25)

4 lemon wedges

~~~~~~~~~~~~~~~~~~~~~~

1 Wash and dry the fish wing but keep it in one piece. Mix the lemon juice, salt and turmeric together then rub it into the fish and leave to stand for 30 minutes.

2 Shake off any excess coating and coat the fish with the red marinade. Again let it stand for 30–60 minutes.

3 To cook, preheat the grill to medium heat. Put the skate on to a rack above a foil-lined grill tray and place this in the midway position under the heat. Alternatively, it can be barbecued.

4 Cook for 12–15 minutes, turning at least once.

5 To finish off, raise the tray nearer to the heat and singe the skate to obtain a little blackening. Cut into four and serve on a bed of salad with lemon wedges, naan bread and tandoori chutney.

Tandoori Pilchard

As an alternative to fresh pilchards you could use other oily fish such as herring or mackerel in this recipe. Or try snapper for a change.

~~~~~~~~~~~~~~~~~~~~~~

Serves 2 as a starter

2 fresh pilchards, about 12 oz (345 g) each

7 oz (200 g) green tandoori marinade (page 26)

~~~~~~~~~~~~~~~~~~~~~~~~~~~~~~

1   Gut and wash the pilchards then dry them. Coat with the marinade and leave for 30–60 minutes.

2   To cook, preheat the grill to high heat. Put the pilchards on to a rack above a foil-lined grill tray and place this in the midway position under the heat. Alternatively, they can be barbecued.

3   Cook for 10–12 minutes, turning at least once.

4   To finish off, raise the tray nearer to the heat and singe the pilchards to obtain a little blackening. Serve on a bed of salad with lemon wedges, naan bread and tandoori chutney.

Tikka Cod Chunks

The white filleted chunks look superb with the red marinade and taste as good as they look.

~~~~~~~~~~~~~~~~~~~~~~~~~~~~~~

Serves 2 as a main course or 4 as a starter

12 oz (350 g) cod fillet steaks, chopped into 1 inch (2.5 cm) cubes

7 oz (200 g) red tandoori marinade (page 25)

~~~~~~~~~~~~~~~~~~~~~~~~~~~~~~

1   In a non-metallic bowl combine the fish chunks and the marinade. Leave to marinate for up to 1 hour.

2   To cook, preheat the grill to high heat. Slide the chunks on to four skewers, leaving a slight gap between each piece. Put the skewers on to a rack above a foil-lined grill tray and place this in the midway position under the heat. Alternatively, they can be barbecued.

3   Grill for about 10 minutes, turning at least once.

4   To finish off, raise the tray nearer to the heat to obtain a little blackening. Serve on a bed of salad with lemon wedges, naan bread and tandoori chutney.

Tikka Monkfish

The ugliest fish in the world is also one of the tastiest and it deserves its name 'poor man's lobster'. Here is a variation on the previous recipe.

~~~~~~~~~~~~~~~~~~~~~~~~

Serves 2 as part of the main course or 4 as a starter

12 oz (350 g) monkfish steaks, filleted, gutted, skinned and cut into 1 inch (2.5 cm) cubes

7 oz (200 g) raan tandoori marinade (page 27)

~~~~~~~~~~~~~~~~~~~~~~~~

To prepare and cook, follow the previous recipe exactly.

Tikka King Prawn

A further variation of the Tikka Cod recipe.

~~~~~~~~~~~~~~~~~~~~~~~~

Serves 4 as a starter or 2 as part of a main course

12 raw king prawns, each weighing about 1 oz (25–30 g) when thawed, shelled, de-veined and cleaned

7 oz (200 g) green tandoori marinade (page 26)

~~~~~~~~~~~~~~~~~~~~~~~~

To prepare and cook, follow the Tikka Cod Chunks recipe on page 59.

Squid Ring Tikka

This variation of the Tikka Cod Chunks recipe makes a superb crispy alternative to Spanish-style calamaris.

~~~~~~~~~~~~~~~~~~~~~~~~~~~~

Serves 2 as part of the main course

12 oz (350 g) pre-prepared squid, cleaned and cut into rings

7 oz (200 g) red tandoori marinade (page 25)

~~~~~~~~~~~~~~~~~~~~~~~~~~~~

To prepare and cook, follow the Tikka Cod Chunks recipe on page 59.

Lobster Tandoori

Expensive, yes, but for that occasional romantic treat, why not? Here it is served as a starter, and to top things off . . . serve it with pink champagne!

~~~~~~~~~~~~~~~~~~~~~~~~~~~~

Serves 2 as a starter

7–8 oz (200–225 g) pre-prepared raw lobster tail flesh, cut into bite-size cubes

7 oz (200 g) red tandoori marinade (see page 25)

~~~~~~~~~~~~~~~~~~~~~~~~~~~~

1 Mix the lobster pieces and the marinade together in a non-metallic mixing bowl. Cover and refrigerate for between 6 and 24 hours.

2 To cook, preheat the oven to 375°F/190°C/Gas 5. Slide the lobster pieces on to skewers, leaving a slight gap between each piece. Put the skewers on to an oven rack above a foil-lined oven tray and place this in the oven. Alternatively, they can be barbecued.

3 Cook for about 15 minutes, turning at least once. Serve on a bed of salad with lemon wedges, naan bread and tandoori chutney.

Tandoori Tiger Prawn

Huge black striped prawns up to 10 inches (25 cm) long, thrive in the Bay of Bengal. Aptly named 'tiger' prawns, they weigh up to 4 oz (110 g) each and though expensive, are superbly fleshy and tasty, and a good fishmonger will supply you with them.

Serves 2 as a starter

2 × 4 oz (110 g) raw Bengal tiger prawns, shelled, de-veined and cleaned

7 oz (200 g) raan tandoori marinade (see page 27)

1 Prick the prawns with a fork and coat thoroughly with the marinade in a non-metallic bowl. Cover and put in the fridge for a maximum of 24 hours.

2 To cook, preheat the grill to medium heat. Slide each prawn on to a skewer. Put the skewer on to a rack above a foil-lined grill tray and place this in the midway position under the heat. Alternatively, they can be barbecued.

3 Cook for 10–12 minutes, turning at least once.

4 To finish off, raise the tray nearer to the heat and singe the prawns to obtain a little blackening. Serve on a bed of salad with lemon wedges, naan bread and tandoori chutney.

Crab Tikka

Crab is very rarely seen at the tandoori house, which is a pity because, in this recipe, it is simple to cook and is simply delicious! It's rich though, so a little goes a long way.

~~~~~~~~~~~~~~~~~~~~~~~~~~~~~~~~~

Serves 2 as a starter

3 oz (75 g) fresh (or frozen) shredded white crab meat

1 oz (25 g) fresh (or frozen) shredded brown crab meat

1 tablespoon red tandoori paste (see page 24)

3 or 4 tablespoons double cream

salt to taste

2 or 3 lemon wedges

~~~~~~~~~~~~~~~~~~~~~~~~~~~~~~~~~

1 Simply mix the crab, paste and cream together in a bowl.

2 You can serve it hot or cold. If hot, stir-fry it in a small frying pan until it is hot. If serving cold, refrigerate for an hour or so. Whichever way you serve it, salt to taste and serve with salad and the lemon wedges.

Crab Tikka Avocado

~~~~~~~~~~~~~~~~~~~~~~~~~~~~~~~~~

Serves 4 as a starter

~~~~~~~~~~~~~~~~~~~~~~~~~~~~~~~~~

Simply halve two avocados, dispose of the stone and fill the holes with the hot crab tikka (see above), covering the whole top face of the avocado. Optionally cover with slices of mozarella cheese and 'flash' the avocados under the grill until the cheese melts.

The avocados can, of course, be filled with cold crab tikka and refrigerated prior to serving. In this case omit the cheese.

Tandoori Clams in Shell

The clam has a hard, hinged double shell similar to oysters, mussels and scallops. It lives in sand and mud flats around coastal waters.

Its first recorded use was in China in the Tang dynasty of the eighth century, when the clams were fished from the Yangtze river. Today they are farmed in the USA and are readily available frozen. Although they are available shelled, I prefer them in their shells. They come in three sizes in their shell: small (averaging 30 to the pound/450 g), medium (20 to the pound) and large (10 to the pound). I specify the medium size below, but you can use the size of your choice.

Clams make excellent tandoori subjects.

Serves 2 as a starter	**some butter**
1 lb (450 g) frozen medium ('*petite* neck') clams	**some chopped chive leaves to garnish**
7 oz (200 g) red tandoori marinade (page 25)	**lemon or lime wedges**

1 Allow the clams to thaw (it will take 2 hours at room temperature).

2 Open the clams discarding any bad ones. Discard half the shells. Wash and set aside the remaining shells (see opposite).

3 Rinse the clams then immerse them in the marinade in a non-metallic bowl. Cover and refrigerate for 2–12 hours.

4 To cook, preheat the grill to medium heat. Line the grill tray with foil and put the grill rack in the tray.

5 Put each clam into a shell half. Distribute the excess marinade into each shell. Top each with a pea-size knob of butter.

6 Put the shells on the rack and place the grill tray under the heat at the midway position. Grill for about 5 minutes (maybe less, maybe more, depending on clam size and grill temperature).

7 Garnish with the chopped chives and serve with lemon or lime wedges on a bed of salad.

Opening clams

You need a special oyster knife (available from cookshops) which has a thick, wide, stubby blunt blade. A wide screwdriver can substitute, but a kitchen knife blade is too thin and is liable to break.

1 Hold the clam in a tea cloth with its shell hinge facing you.

2 Insert the blade near the hinge, wiggle and twist until the hinge separates. Separate the two halves of the shell.

3 Run the blade all around the shell half containing the flesh to cut the muscle away from the shell.

4 Discard only clams which are dried up, off-colour or are bubbled.

Tandoori Scallops in Shell au gratin

The scallop is a British native and is also found worldwide in seas and oceans. Like clams, oysters and mussels, the scallop has a hard, hinged double shell. The shell itself is ribbed, flattish and relatively large and is often tinged with coral pink. The shells are pretty enough to be used to serve the scallops on, and although generally the scallops are sold frozen without shells, most fishmongers will supply shells if required.

Scallops come in three sizes: small (30–40 per kilo/2.2 lb), medium (20–30 per kilo) and large (10–20 per kilo). Four small, three medium or two large is ample per person for a starter.

Scallops contain white meat (the round muscle) which is attached to a creamy white and coral pink roe, known as the 'foot'. All this is edible. The gut and gill should have already been removed by the fishmonger.

The pink of the roe and the shell are greatly enhanced by the pink of the tandoori marinade.

~~~~~~~~~~~~~~~~~~~~~~~~~~~~~~

Serves 2 as a starter

**6 medium-sized scallops,
thawed if frozen**

**7 oz (200 g) red tandoori
marinade (page 25)**

some butter

**2 oz (50 g) grated Cheddar
cheese (optional)**

lime wedges

**some chopped chive leaves
to garnish**

~~~~~~~~~~~~~~~~~~~~~~~~~~~~~~

1   Rinse the scallops well then follow the clam recipe on page 63 from stage 3 to its end.

2   If you wish to create an 'au gratin' crust – which does suit this dish well – place equal amounts of the grated cheese on each scallop after they have cooked for 4 minutes. Return to the heat and finish off for a couple more minutes.

Scallop Tikka

Scallops work really well on skewers. Here I use small scallops, each weighing about 1 oz (25 g).

~~~~~~~~~~~~~~~~~~~~~~~~~~~~~~

Serves 2 as a starter

8–10 small scallops, thawed if frozen

7 oz (200 g) red tandoori marinade (page 25)

~~~~~~~~~~~~~~~~~~~~~~~~~~~~~~

1   In a non-metallic bowl combine the scallops and the marinade. Leave to marinate for up to 1 hour.

2   To cook, preheat the grill to high heat. Slide the scallops on to two skewers, leaving a slight gap between each piece. Put the skewers on a rack above a foil-lined grill tray and place this in the midway position under the heat. Alternatively, they can be barbecued.

3 Grill for 4–5 minutes, turning frequently.

Piri Piri Prawn Tikka

Strictly for the heat lovers, this is a red-hot chilli marinade from Goa, with a hint of tandoori flavouring but with no yoghurt. I particularly like this garnished with finely chopped green chilli rings. Here I am using king prawns, but you can use this marinade for any of the tikka recipes in this book. Simply substitute this one for the standard tandoori marinade. Note the optional extra hot chilli powder for real heat lovers.

~~~~~~~~~~~~~~~~~~~~

Serves 2 as a starter

8–12 raw king prawns, each weighing ½–¾ oz (15–20 g)

Marinade
6–10 fresh red cayenne, habanero or Scotch bonnet chillies, chopped

2 tablespoons tomato ketchup

4 tablespoons olive oil

2 tablespoons fresh lime juice

3 or 4 garlic cloves, chopped

2 teaspoons coriander seeds, roasted and ground

1 teaspoon mild curry paste (page 21)

1 tablespoon red tandoori paste (page 24)

1 or more teaspoons extra hot chilli powder (optional)

~~~~~~~~~~~~~~~~~~~~

1 Put all the marinade ingredients into the blender and pulse it into as fine a purée as you can get, using a little water to achieve a dropping consistency.

2 In a non-metallic bowl combine the king prawns and the marinade, cover and refrigerate for up to 24 hours.

3 To cook, preheat the grill to high heat. Slide the prawns on to two skewers, leaving a slight gap between each prawn. Put the skewers on to a rack above a foil-lined grill tray and place this in the midway position under the heat. Alternatively, they can be barbecued.

4 Cook for about 10 minutes, turning at least once. To finish off, raise the tray nearer to the heat to obtain a little blackening. Serve on a bed of salad with some lemon wedges, naan bread and tandoori chutney.

CHAPTER 5

Vegetables

Traditionally only meat or poultry was cooked in the tandoor. Vegetables were never considered worthy. Indeed you will rarely, if ever, find them in the tandoori restaurant. More's the pity, because as the following recipes prove, there are as many delicious tandoori tikka-style vegetable dishes as there are vegetables.

I have adapted a tikka recipe for vegetables by using a quick stir-fry technique. The tandoor (or conventional oven or grill) is a little too violent to achieve the subtlety of texture and moisture needed, and the stir-fry works well. Amongst the examples I give, are such diverse vegetables as mangetout, mooli, sweetcorn, carrot, parsnip, asparagus, mushroom and chestnut.

You can, of course, apply the technique to any vegetable of your choice. A surprisingly interesting recipe is pineapple tikka, and the chapter ends with a favourite of mine, paneer (not a vegetable at all but a type of Indian cheese) – in this case on skewers, cooked tikka-style.

Tandoori Baked Potato

One of the best vegetable adaptations to tandoori-style is the potato (and its close relatives, the yam, sweet potato, swede, parsnip and turnip). It is tandoori-marinated then foil wrapped and slow baked.

~~~~~~~~~~~~~~~~~~~

Serves 2 as a snack or to accompany a meal

2 large baking potatoes

7 oz (200 g) tandoori marinade, red, green or raan (pages 25–27)

~~~~~~~~~~~~~~~~~~~

1   Scrub and peel the potatoes, then poke them deeply with a small thin-bladed knife to assist the marinade to penetrate. Immerse them in the marinade in a non-metallic bowl, cover and refrigerate for up to 24 hours.

2   To cook, preheat the oven to 325°F/160°C/Gas 3. Ensure each potato is liberally coated with marinade, then double wrap them carefully in foil. Keep the spare marinade for later.

3   Place the potatoes on an oven tray and bake for 1–1¼ hours.

4   Before unwrapping, test that they are cooked by poking a skewer through each potato. If there is no resistance they are cooked.

5   When cooked, unwrap the potatoes and, keeping them on their foil, pour over the spare marinade. Put them under a medium grill to finish them off – just cook them until they blacken a little bit, turning once. Serve hot, on a bed of salad, with chutney and Indian breads.

Some Variations

Try ringing the changes by using other roots and tubers such as small white yam, red sweet potato (American yam), white sweet potato, parsnip, swede, turnip, even uncooked beetroot. Choose a size which you consider is sufficient per person, and follow the previous recipe, adjusting the cooking time to suit the type and size of vegetable (yams, sweet potatoes and parsnip, for example, will take less time than potatoes of the same size).

Roast Tikka Potato

The Great British roast potato is a hero amongst dishes, transforming the ubiquitous potato into a world-class edible. Add tandoori marinade and it becomes even more sumptuous, especially when served with tandoori roasts (see index). They can be roasted in ghee or vegetable oil, but ghee gives the best flavour.

Choose your potatoes by eye. For roasting they should be neither too big nor too small. Between 2–2½ inches (5–6.5 cm) diameter is ideal. Allow a minimum of 2, maximum of 3 potatoes per person.

~~~~~~~~~~~~~~~~~~~~~~~~

Serves 4 as an accompaniment

8–12 potatoes (see above)

7 oz (200 g) tandoori marinade – red, green or raan (pages 25–27)

sufficient ghee or vegetable oil to cover the bottom of your oven tray

~~~~~~~~~~~~~~~~~~~~~~~~

1 Scrub and peel the potatoes. Halve them and prick them deeply all over. Place the marinade in a large non-metallic bowl and immerse the potatoes in it. Cover and refrigerate for up to 24 hours.

2 Preheat the oven to 400°F/200°C/Gas 6. Put the ghee or oil on to an oven tray and warm it in the hot oven for 5 minutes or so.

3 Shake excess marinade off the potatoes, and keep for later. Remove the hot oven tray and place the potatoes on it. Return the tray to the oven.

4 After 20 minutes turn the potatoes over and baste with the ghee or oil. Add any remaining marinade.

5 They should be ready after a further 25–30 minutes. If cooking

with a roast main dish, time the potatoes so they have a minimum of 45 minutes.

Some Variations

Small white yam, red sweet potato (American yam), white sweet potato, parsnip, swede and turnip can be roasted using exactly the same recipe as above. Adjust the cooking times accordingly (yams, sweet potatoes and parsnips will require less time than potatoes).

Tikka Dry Stir-fry Vegetables

This technique enables you to stir-fry virtually any vegetable to completion in just a few minutes. The use of the tandoori marinade gives the vegetables a distinctive, tasty unusual flavour. The choice of vegetables is up to you, but I give suggestions in the recipes on pages 74–75.

~~~~~~~~~~~~~~~~~~~~~~~~~~~~~~

Serves 4 as an accompaniment dish

1 lb (450 g) prepared vegetables of your choice (see pages 74–75)

2 tablespoons ghee or vegetable oil

2 garlic cloves, sliced

1 inch (2.5 cm) cube ginger, sliced (optional)

4 oz (110 g) onion, sliced

3–4 tablespoons tandoori marinade (red, green or raan, pages 25–27)

2–3 tomatoes, chopped

a few pieces green and/or red pepper, chopped

0–2 fresh chillies (red and/or green), chopped

salt to taste

1–2 teaspoons garam masala (page 18)

Spices
1 teaspoon white cummin seeds

½ teaspoon black cummin seeds (optional)

½ teaspoon wild onion seeds

½ teaspoon black mustard seeds

~~~~~~~~~~~~~~~~~~~~~~~~~~~~~~

1 Heat the ghee or oil in a large karahi or wok.

2 Fry the **spices** for 20 seconds then add the garlic and stir-fry for 30 seconds more. Add the optional ginger and continue stir-frying for 30 seconds more. Add the onions and, lowering the heat, fry for about 5 minutes to allow them to begin to go golden, stirring occasionally.

3 While onion is cooking, blanch the vegetables in boiling water (or steam or microwave them) just to heat and soften them.

4 When the onions are starting to turn golden, raise the heat and add the marinade. Stir-fry the mixture for a couple of minutes, until it changes colour (goes darker), meaning it is cooked.

5 Add the softened vegetables to the stir-fry with the tomatoes, peppers and chillies and stir-fry for just a few minutes until they are as crisp or tender as you want them. If at any time the dish starts sticking, add a little water to 'release' (but not swamp) it. Salt to taste, sprinkle with the garam masala and serve at once.

Stir-fried vegetables

The five recipes on this and the following page demonstrate what a wide variety of vegetables can be cooked using the stir-fry method on page 72. Feel free to use any other vegetables, or combinations of vegetables, of your choice

Mangetout, Mooli and Sweetcorn Tikka Stir-fry

~~~~~~~~~~~~~~~~~~~~~~~~~~~~~

Serves 4 as an accompaniment

6 oz (175 g) fresh mangetout, topped and tailed

5 oz (150 g) mooli (white radish), chopped into bite-sized pieces

5 oz (150 g) fresh or frozen sweetcorn kernels

remaining ingredients as in the recipe on page 72

~~~~~~~~~~~~~~~~~~~~~~~~~~~~~

To cook, follow the previous recipe on page 72 exactly.

Carrot and Parsnip Tikka Stir-fry

~~~~~~~~~~~~~~~~~~~~~~~~~~~~~

Serves 4 as an accompaniment

8 oz (225 g) carrot, peeled and chopped into bite-sized pieces

8 oz (225 g) parsnips, chopped into bite-sized pieces

remaining ingredients as in the recipe on page 72

~~~~~~~~~~~~~~~~~~~~~~~~~~~~~

To cook, follow the recipe on page 72, making sure that the parsnips and carrots are softened in stage 3.

Asparagus Tikka Stir-fry

~~~~~~~~~~~~~~~~~~~~~

Serves 4 as an accompaniment

1 lb (450 g) fresh asparagus, weighed after trimming

**remaining ingredients as in the recipe on page 72,
omitting the tomato, peppers and chilli if you wish**

~~~~~~~~~~~~~~~~~~~~~

Follow the recipe on page 72. To soften the asparagus in stage 3,
I find the microwave creates the least fuss. Simply place the
asparagus in a large enough dish with an inch (2.5 cm) of water
in it and run the microwave for 3–4 minutes on full heat (650
watt).

Mushroom Tikka Stir-fry

~~~~~~~~~~~~~~~~~~~~~

Serves 4 as an accompaniment

1 lb (450 g) mushrooms, any type

remaining ingredients as in the recipe on page 72

~~~~~~~~~~~~~~~~~~~~~

Follow the recipe on page 72. There is no need to blanch or soften
the mushrooms in stage 3. Simply clean and peel them if required,
and add them after the marinade has changed colour.

Chestnut Tikka Stir-fry

~~~~~~~~~~~~~~~~~~~~~

Serves 4 as an accompaniment

**1 lb (450 g) peeled, cooked chestnuts, fresh,
canned and drained or vacuum packed**

remaining ingredients as in the recipe on page 72

~~~~~~

Follow the recipe on page 72, omitting stage 3.

Pineapple (Ananas) Tikka

Pineapples (ananas) were first brought to India from South America by the early sixteenth-century Portuguese. The Emperor Akbar liked them enough to have them grown in the royal gardens at his Agra red fort. Today pineapples are grown prolifically all over India.

This astonishing concept of tandooring pineapple chunks comes from Chef Cyrus, owner of London's Namaste Restaurant in Prescot Street, E1.

Use only fresh pineapple as canned pieces are too soft and too wet.

~~~~~~

Serves 2 as a starter

8–10 chunky pieces fresh pineapple, cut into 1½ inch (4 cm) cubes

7 oz (200 g) red tandoori marinade (page 25)

~~~~~~

1   Place the pineapple and marinade in a non-metallic bowl. Cover and refrigerate for 24–60 hours.

2   Just prior to cooking, thread the pineapple pieces on to two skewers. (Use any spare marinade in a curry.) Preheat the grill to medium.

3   Place the skewers on a rack above the foil-lined grill tray and place this in the midway position. Alternatively they can be barbecued. Cook for 5 minutes, turn over and cook for a further 5 minutes.

4   When fully cooked, raise the tray nearer to the heat and singe the pieces to obtain a little blackening. Serve on a bed of salad with lemon wedges, naan bread and tandoori chutney.

Paneer

Paneer is easy-to-make Indian cheese. You need rather a lot of milk to make it, but the liquid left at the end (the whey) can be used for soups or stock. You'll need up to 2 hours to make the paneer (mostly waiting time) so plan in advance. For recipes using paneer, see below and page 78.

~~~~~~~~~~~~~~~~~~~~~~~~~~~~

Makes 16 cubes

4 pints (2.25 litres) full cream milk (not UHT)

4–6 tablespoons vinegar, any type, or lemon juice

~~~~~~~~~~~~~~~~~~~~~~~~~~~~

1 Bring the milk slowly to the boil in a large pan.

2 Add the vinegar or lemon juice, stirring until it curdles.

3 When the curds separate from the whey, strain through a clean tea towel placed on a strainer over a saucepan.

4 Fold the tea towel over and press through the excess liquid – the whey. Keep for later use as stock.

5 Now place the curds – from now on called **paneer** – on to the draining board, still in the tea towel. Press it out to a circle about ½ inch (1–2 cm) thick.

6 Place a flat weight (the original saucepan full of water for instance) on the tea towel and allow it to compress the paneer.

7 If you want **crumbly paneer**, remove the weight after 30 to 45 minutes and crumble the paneer.

8 If you want the paneer to be solid, keep the weight on for 1½–2 hours. Then cut the paneer into 16 cubes.

Paneer Tikka on Skewers

This is one of my favourite tikka recipes. As usual, the paneer cubes are marinated, skewered and grilled.

~~~~~~~~~~~~~~~~~~~~~~~~~~~

Serves 2 as a starter

7 oz (200 g) red tandoori marinade (page 25)

16 cubes paneer (page 77)

8 pieces green pepper (the same size as the paneer)

8 pieces onion (the same size as the paneer)

lemon wedges

salad

~~~~~~~~~~~~~~~~~~~~~~~~~~~

1   In a non-metallic bowl, combine the marinade with the paneer cubes. Cover and refrigerate for 6 hours.

2   To cook, preheat the grill to medium. Intersperse eight pieces of paneer on a skewer with the green pepper and onion pieces. Repeat with a second skewer.

3   Place the skewers on an oven rack above a foil-lined oven tray. Place this in the midway position under the grill. Alternatively they can be barbecued.

4   Turn the skewers and cook for a further 3 minutes. Serve with lemon wedges on a bed of salad.

CHAPTER 6

Tandoori and Tikka Masala Curries

These curries have no history of authenticity in the sub-continent of India, nor in Pakistan where tandoori and tikka originated. They are in fact one of the few innovative dishes created by the British curry house.

My first encounter with the concept was around 1978 or 1980, after the tandoori invasion in the seventies (see page x). It was still a new thing then. But just who thought of it, where and when, is not on record. Whoever did should have been on royalties, for he or she invented the world's most popular curry.

The concept is so simple. Make tandoori or tikka 'something' (meat, chicken, fish etc) and serve it in a complementary creamy, rich, red tangy sauce, made in the typical curry house way, but coloured with tandoori/tikka paste and red tomatoes and peppers.

My version omits the tartrazine red food colouring used by curry houses, and is therefore not as lurid as the equivalent restaurant curries. (You can add it if you wish, see pages 12 and 20.) It is, however, supremely tasty.

We start with the basic curry gravy or sauce, and follow with a number of Tandoori and Tikka recipes.

Tikka/Tandoori Masala Curry Gravy

Tikka/tandoori masala gravy is a relatively recent UK curry house invention, which has become so popular that it is even to be found on the menus of the better restaurants in Bombay and Delhi. It is a curry master sauce or gravy which is spiced in the tandoori style and should be a gorgeous reddish colour. It can be used in its own right as a gravy, or it can be used to make dryish tikka/tandoori dishes into a tikka masala curry, for example in the recipes on pages 81, 82 and 86–90.

~~~~~~~~~~~~~~~~

Makes about 16 oz (450 g) gravy

2 tablespoons vegetable oil

2 garlic cloves, minced

4 oz (110 g) onion, very finely chopped

1 tablespoon mild curry paste (page 21)

1 tablespoon red tandoori paste (page 24)

4 canned plum tomatoes

1 tablespoon vinegar, any type

1 tablespoon tomato ketchup

6 fl oz (175 ml) canned tomato soup

½ green pepper, chopped

0–4 green chillies (optional)

3 fl oz (75 ml) single cream

2 tablespoons coconut milk powder (optional)

1 tablespoon garam masala (page 18)

1 tablespoon dried fenugreek leaf

1 tablespoon chopped fresh coriander

salt to taste

~~~~~~~~~~~~~~~~

1   Heat the oil in a large karahi or wok. Stir-fry the garlic for 30 seconds, add the onion and stir-fry for 8–10 minutes.

2   Add the pastes and stir-fry for a couple of minutes.

3 Add the tomatoes, vinegar, ketchup, soup, green pepper and chillies. Simmer and stir-fry for 5 minutes or so.

4 Add the remaining ingredients except the salt and simmer for a further 5 minutes, adding water as needed to maintain a gravy consistency. Salt to taste.

Note: For those who like it spicier, add a tablespoon more of the tandoori paste and as much chilli powder as you wish at stage 2.

Meat Tikka Masala Curry

A popular and tasty curry, well worth the effort to make it. You will need to make one recipe of Meat Tikka (see page 31) before you begin.

~~~~~~~~~~~~~~~

Serves 4
3 tablespoons vegetable oil

4 garlic cloves, minced

8 oz (225 g) onions, very finely chopped

1 tablespoon mild curry paste (page 21)

2 tablespoons red tandoori paste (page 24)

1 tablespoon green masala paste (page 22)

6 canned plum tomatoes

2 tablespoons vinegar, any type

1 tablespoon tomato ketchup

6 oz (175 g) canned tomato soup

½ green pepper, chopped

0–4 green chillies (optional)

20–24 meat tikka pieces, cooked to the recipe on page 31

4 fl oz (100 ml) single cream

1 tablespoon garam masala (page 18)

1 tablespoon chopped fresh coriander

salt to taste

~~~~~~~~~~~~~~~

1 Heat the vegetable oil in a large karahi or wok. Stir-fry the garlic

for 30 seconds, add the onion and stir-fry for 8–10 minutes until golden brown.

2 Add the pastes and stir-fry for a couple of minutes.

3 Add the tomatoes, vinegar, ketchup, soup, green pepper and chillies and, when simmering, the meat tikka pieces.

4 Stir-fry for about 5 minutes then add the cream, garam masala and coriander. Simmer for a further 10 minutes, or until the meat is as tender as you like it, adding enough water as needed to maintain a nice gravy consistency. Salt to taste and serve.

Liver Tikka Masala

Liver Tikka (page 41) can easily become Liver Tikka Masala Curry by adding it and any spare marinade to a full portion (16 oz/450 g) of cooked tikka/tandoori masala gravy (see page 80). Cook the gravy first, and keep it warm or reheat it to coincide with the timing of your tikka ingredients.

Serves 4

1 lb (450 g) lamb's liver, chopped into 1 inch (2.5 cm) cubes

7 oz (200 g) red tandoori marinade (page 25)

4 tablespoons ghee or vegetable oil

1 teaspoon cummin seeds

16 oz (450 g) tikka/tandoori masala gravy (page 80)

1 In a non-metallic bowl, mix the liver with the marinade. Cover and refrigerate for 6–24 hours.

2 Heat the ghee or oil in a large karahi or wok. Add the cummin seeds, then the liver pieces, shaking off any excess marinade. Stir-fry for 5–8 minutes.

3 Meanwhile, reheat the tikka/tandoori masala gravy.

4 Combine the gravy with the liver in the wok, adding any excess marinade from stage 2. Simmer until the liver is cooked.

Tandoori Keema Masala Curry

Minced beef is cheap and easy to cook. It is perfect for tandoori-style curry, as this recipe proves.

~~~~~~~~~~~~~~~

Serves 4

3 tablespoons vegetable oil

2 garlic cloves, very finely chopped

6 oz (175 g) onion, very finely chopped

1 tablespoon mild curry paste (page 21)

1 tablespoon red tandoori paste (page 24)

1½ lb (675 g) lean minced beef

6 cherry tomatoes, chopped

1 tablespoon tomato purée

1 tablespoon mango chutney, finely chopped

5 fl oz (150 ml) canned tomato soup

½ red pepper, chopped

stock or water, as needed

1 tablespoon garam masala (page 18)

4 fl oz (100 ml) single cream

1 tablespoon chopped fresh coriander leaves

salt to taste

~~~~~~~~~~~~~~~

1 Preheat the oven to 375°F/190°C/Gas 5.

2 Heat the oil in a karahi or wok and add the garlic and onion and the pastes. Stir-fry for 10 minutes.

3 Add the mince and stir-fry for 5–10 minutes.

4 Transfer it all to a 4½ pint (2.6 litre) lidded casserole, adding the tomatoes, purée, chutney, soup and red pepper. Stir well, put the lid on and place in the hot oven.

5 After about 20 minutes, stir and add a little stock or water if needed, to prevent it sticking.

6 Continue to cook for another 20 minutes, then add the garam masala, cream and the fresh coriander and cook for at least 10 more minutes.

7   Just prior to serving, spoon off any excess oil and add salt to taste.

Chicken Tikka Masala

At the Tandoori restaurant, chicken is by far the most popular main
ingredient and chicken tikka masala, a pure restaurant invention
(and a brilliant one) is by far the most popular restaurant dish.

~~~~~~~~~~~~~~~~~~~~~~~~

Serves 2–3

2 tablespoons vegetable oil

3 garlic cloves, minced

8 oz (225 g) onion, very finely chopped

1½ tablespoons mild curry paste (page 21)

1½ tablespoons red tandoori paste (page 24)

1 tablespoon green masala paste (page 22)

6 canned plum tomatoes

1 tablespoon vinegar, any type

1 tablespoon tomato ketchup

6 fl oz (175 ml) canned tomato soup

½ green pepper, chopped

0–4 green chillies (optional)

20–24 chicken tikka pieces, cooked to the recipe on page 52

4 fl oz (100 ml) single cream

1 tablespoon garam masala (page 18)

1 tablespoon chopped fresh coriander

salt to taste

~~~~~~~~~~~~~~~~~~~~~~~~

1   Heat the oil in a large karahi or wok.

2   Stir-fry the garlic for 30 seconds, then add the onion and stir-fry
for 8–10 minutes until golden brown.

3   Add the pastes and stir-fry for a couple of minutes.

4   Add the tomatoes, vinegar, ketchup, soup, green pepper and
chillies. Stir-fry for 5 minutes or so, then add the chicken, cream,
garam masala and coriander. Simmer for a further 5 minutes,
adding a little water if it needs it. Salt to taste and serve.

Chicken Makhanwalla

A whole chicken is tandooried then jointed, and finished off in a tasty, spicy red gravy topped with a butter tarka, the *makhanwalla*.

〰〰〰〰〰〰〰〰〰

Serves 4 as part of the main course

1 × 3½–3¾ lb (1.5–1.75 kg) roasting chicken

juice of 3 lemons

1 lb 5 oz (600 g) red tandoori marinade (page 25)

2 tablespoons butter ghee

4 garlic cloves, finely chopped

8 oz (225 g) onion, very finely chopped

1 tablespoon mild curry paste (page 21)

2 tablespoons red tandoori paste (page 24)

8 canned plum tomatoes

6 fl oz (150 ml) canned tomato soup

1 tablespoon tomato purée

salt to taste

Tarka

3 tablespoons butter

2 tablespoons dried onion flakes

1 tablespoon garam masala (page 18)

1 tablespoon chopped fresh coriander leaves

2 fresh red chillies, chopped (optional)

Spices

1 teaspoon cummin seeds

½ teaspoon fennel seeds

½ teaspoon cardamom seeds

Garnish

a curl of single cream

roasted almond flakes

whole fresh coriander leaves and/or fresh mint leaves, shredded

〰〰〰〰〰〰〰〰〰

1 Skin the chicken, clean it inside and out, and gash the flesh with the tip of a sharp knife. Rub it all over with the lemon juice, and leave it to dry for 30 minutes.

2 In a large non-metallic bowl, combine the chicken and the marinade. Cover and refrigerate for 24–60 hours (see page 24).

3 To cook, pre-heat the oven to 350°F/180°C/Gas 4.

4 Shake off and keep the considerable excess marinade and put the chicken into a large casserole dish. Put it into the oven without the lid and bake for 30 minutes.

5 During this time, heat the ghee in a karahi and stir-fry the spices for 30 seconds.

6 Add the garlic, and 30 seconds later add the onions and reduce the heat. Stir-fry for about 15 minutes.

7 Add the pastes and stir them in for a couple of minutes, then add the tomatoes, canned soup and purée and the excess marinade. Simmer for at least 15 minutes.

8 Remove the chicken from the oven and joint it into 8 pieces (2 thighs, 2 drumsticks, 2 wings and 2 back pieces).

9 Return these pieces, with the simmering sauce, to the casserole. Mix well. Put the lid on and bake for 20 minutes.

10 In the karahi, heat the butter and stir-fry the tarka ingredients for 2–3 minutes. Place them on top of the chicken, and cook in the oven for a final 10–20 minutes, with the lid off. Salt to taste, garnish and serve.

Cod Tikka Masala Curry

Tikka cod chunks (page 59) can easily become a tikka/tandoori masala curry by adding it and any spare marinade to a full portion (16 oz/450 g) of cooked tikka/tandoori masala gravy (page 80). Cook the gravy first, and keep it warm or reheat it to coincide with the timing of your tikka ingredients.

Serves 2 as part of the main course

12 oz (350 g) cod fillet steaks, cut into cubes and cooked following the tikka cod recipe on page 59

16 oz (450 g) tikka/tandoori masala curry gravy (page 80), hot

fresh whole coriander leaves to garnish

Combine the freshly cooked tikka cod chunks with the hot gravy. Garnish with fresh coriander leaves and serve.

Monkfish Tikka Masala Curry

Tikka monkfish (page 60) can easily become a tikka/tandoori masala curry by adding it and any spare marinade to a full portion (16 oz/450 g) of hot tikka/tandoori masala gravy (page 80). Cook the gravy first, and keep it warm or reheat it to coincide with the cooking of the tikka monkfish.

Tiger Prawn Tandoori Masala Curry

Tandoori tiger prawn (page 62) can easily become a tikka/tandoori masala curry by adding it and any spare marinade to a full portion (16 oz/450 g) of hot tikka/tandoori masala gravy (page 80). Cook the gravy first, and keep it warm or reheat it to coincide with the cooking of the tiger prawns.

King Prawn Tikka Masala Curry

Tikka king prawn (page 60) can easily become a tikka/tandoori masala curry by adding it and any spare marinade to a full portion (16 oz/450 g) of hot tikka/tandoori masala gravy (page 80). Cook the gravy first, and keep it warm or reheat it to coincide with the cooking of the prawns.

Lobster Tandoori Masala Curry

Lobster tandoori (page 61) can easily become a tikka/tandoori masala curry by adding it and any spare marinade to a full portion (16 oz/450 g) of hot tikka/tandoori masala gravy (page 80). Cook the gravy first, and keep it warm or reheat it to coincide with the cooking of the Lobster tandoori.

Squid Tikka Masala Curry

Squid ring tikka (page 60) can easily become a tikka/tandoori masala curry by adding it and any spare marinade to a full portion (16 oz/450 g) of hot tikka/tandoori masala gravy (page 80). Cook the gravy first, and keep it warm or reheat it to coincide with the cooking of the squid ring tikka.

Brown Shrimp Tikka Masala

The traditional British way of buying fresh whole shrimps (or prawns, which are the same things) is to buy them from the fishmongers by the pint. (For the metric minded this is 600 ml.) Selling by volume allows for considerable variation in density and water content. To be consistent, this recipe weighs tiny brown shrimps which are then cooked with head off but shell on. Everything is edible. The soft shells give a slight crunch and the tikka fry adds a highly complementary taste factor.

~~~~~~~~~~~~~~

Serves 4 as a starter, 2 as part of the main course

3 tablespoons vegetable ghee or oil

3–4 garlic cloves, sliced

1 inch (2.5 cm) cube fresh ginger, finely chopped (optional)

4 oz (110 g) onion, sliced

3–4 tablespoons red tandoori marinade (page 25)

1½ lb (675 g) small raw brown shrimps, head off, shell on

2–3 tomatoes, chopped

a few pieces green and/or red pepper, chopped

0–2 fresh chillies, red and/or green, chopped

salt to taste

1–2 teaspoons garam masala (page 18)

Spices

1 teaspoon white cummin seeds

1 teaspoon sesame seeds

½ teaspoon lovage seeds

~~~~~~~~~~~~~~

1   Heat the ghee or oil in a large karahi or wok.

2   Fry the **spices** for 20 seconds then add the garlic and stir-fry for 30 seconds more.

3   Add the optional ginger and continue stir-frying for 30 seconds more, then add the onions and lower the heat. Fry for about 5 minutes to allow them to begin to go golden, stirring occasionally.

4   Raise the heat, add the marinade and stir-fry the mixture for a couple of minutes, until it changes colour (goes darker) meaning it is cooked.

5   Add the shrimps, tomatoes, peppers and chillies and stir-fry for 5–8 minutes until they are cooked. If at any time the dish starts sticking, add a little water to 'release' (but not swamp) it. Salt to taste, sprinkle with the garam masala and serve at once.

Aloo Tikka Masala Curry

New potatoes cooked in a rich red creamy sauce that goes well with dry tikka dishes.

Serves 4 as an accompaniment

12 oz (350 g) baby new potatoes, the smaller the better

ingredients to make 16 oz (450 g) tikka/tandoori masala gravy (page 80)

fresh coriander and/or mint leaves, chopped

1   Par-boil the potatoes until about three-quarters cooked.

2   Make the masala gravy following the recipe on page 80, but add the par-cooked potatoes in stage 3, with the tomatoes. Follow the recipe to its end. Serve garnished with freshly chopped coriander or mint leaves.

Mixed Vegetables Tikka Masala Curry

Any vegetables can be used for this curry, but I've chosen frozen mixed vegetables for convenience.

~~~~~~~~~~~~~~~~~~~~~~~~

Serves 4 as an accompaniment

ingredients to make 16 oz (450 g) tikka/tandoori masala gravy, (page 80)

16 oz (450 g) frozen mixed vegetables, thawed

fresh coriander and/or mint leaves, chopped

some shredded fresh or desiccated coconut

~~~~~~~~~~~~~~~~~~~~~~~~

1 Make the tikka masala curry gravy by following the recipe on page 80, but add the vegetables in stage 4 with the cream. Salt to taste, garnish and serve.

2 Follow the recipe to its end, then garnish with freshly chopped coriander or mint leaves and some shredded coconut.

Paneer Tikka Masala Curry

It is nothing like as hard as it might seem creating this magnificent non-meat curry. Serve as part of a main course with other curries, rice and bread.

~~~~~~~~~~~~~~~~~~~~~~~~

Serves 2 as part of the main course

16 cubes paneer (see page 77)

7 oz (200 g) red tandoori marinade (page 25)

16 oz (450 g) tikka/tandoori

masala gravy (see page 80)

1–2 tablespoons cream, optional

fresh coriander leaves, chopped

a few fried almond flakes

~~~~~~~~~~~~~~~~~~~~~~~~

1. Place the paneer cubes and red tandoori marinade in a large non-metallic bowl. Combine well, then cover and refrigerate for about 6 hours.

2. To cook the paneer, preheat the grill. Meanwhile, thread the paneer cubes on to two skewers.

3. Place the skewers on a rack above a foil-lined grill tray and place this in the midway position under the heat grill. Cook for 4 minutes, then turn the skewers and cook for a further 3 minutes. Reheat the gravy in a large saucepan.

4. When the paneer is cooked, remove from the skewers and add to the simmering gravy. Simmer for a minute or two.

5. Garnish with a curl of cream, fresh whole coriander leaves and a sprinkle of fried almond flakes.

Egg Tikka Masala Curry

Hard-boiled eggs make a pleasant change in a curry. Use small (grade 4 or 5) hen's eggs or, for a really interesting dish, use quail's eggs.

Serves 4 as an accompaniment

8 small hens' eggs or 24 quails' eggs

ingredients to make 16 oz (450 g) tikka/tandoori masala gravy (page 80)

salt to taste

fresh coriander and/or mint leaves, chopped

some almond flakes

1. Hard-boil the eggs (15 minutes for hens' eggs, 4 minutes for quails' eggs). Remove the shells when cool enough to handle and cut each egg in half.

2. Make the tikka masala gravy following the recipe on page 80, but add the eggs to the gravy in stage 4 with the cream.

3 Follow the recipe to its end, add salt to taste then garnish with freshly chopped coriander or mint leaves and some almond flakes and serve.

Tikka Masala Sauce For Pasta

At first this is a really strange combination of concepts. But, believe me, it is popular at the supermarket and yes, it actually works.

The sauce goes well with spaghetti, macaroni, lasagne, conchiglie (shells) or in fact any pasta of your choice.

Simply cook your pasta as normal and warm up some tikka/tandoori/masala gravy (page 80). Pour the hot gravy over the pasta, grind over some black pepper and garnish with chopped fresh chillies and some grated Cheddar cheese.

CHAPTER 7

Restaurant Favourite Curries

It was an obvious move for the curry house to advance from the tandoori and tikka masala curry to all types of restaurant favourite curries emanating from the tandoor.

And, of course, it shows how popular tikka tastes are. In this chapter I have given recipes for the most popular restaurant curries which are suitable for the tikka process. These include, in alphabetical order, tikka bhoona (a dryish medium curry), tikka Ceylon (with the contrasts of hot chilli and mild coconut), tikka dhansak (with a lentil purée base), tikka jal frezi (a splendid stir-fry spiked with chilli), tikka kofta (using sheek kebab meat balls), tikka korma (mild, rich and aromatic), tikka moghlai (even more rich and creamy), tikka patia (red, sweet, sour and hot), tikka-rhogan josh (deep red and aromatic), tikka sag gosht (with spinach), and last but not least, tikka vindaloo (the hottest curry in this book).

First you cook the main ingredient tikka-style (choose from the meat, chicken, fish or vegetable tikka recipes in chapters 2–5) then it is simmered in tikka masala gravy, and enhanced with selected spices and flavourings. It requires a little more time and effort, but the results are well worth it.

Tikka Bhoona Curry

The bhoona is a fundamental cooking method involving the frying of ingredients. Because minimal liquid is involved, the ultimate texture of the dish is quite dry. To achieve this we use about half the quantity of tikka/tandoori masala curry gravy (page 80) than we would use for a standard curry. An extra savoury bouquet is given with the addition of cooked crispy onion towards the end of the cooking. (Dehydrated fried onion flakes are available in most supermarkets.)

~~~~~~~~~~

Serves 4

1 tablespoon ghee or vegetable oil

2–3 garlic cloves, finely chopped

2 tablespoons mild curry paste (page 21)

1½ lb (675 g) cooked (hot or cold) tikka of your choice, (tikka meat, poultry, fish or vegetables from chapters 2–5)

8 oz (225 g) cooked tikka/tandoori masala curry gravy (page 80)

1 tablespoon ground almonds

2 teaspoons garam masala (page 18)

4 tablespoons dehydrated fried onion flakes

salt to taste

some fresh coriander leaves to garnish

Spices (roasted and crushed)

1 teaspoon white cummin seeds

1 teaspoon coriander seeds

1 teaspoon sesame seeds

~~~~~~~~~~

1 Heat the oil in the karahi. Stir-fry the spices for 30 seconds then stir-fry the garlic for 30 seconds. Add the curry paste and stir-fry for a further minute.

2 Add the tikka of your choice and briskly stir-fry for about 2 minutes.

3 Stir in the tikka/tandoori masala curry gravy and bring it to the simmer.

4 Add the ground almonds, garam masala, onion flakes and salt to taste and simmer until it is cooked to your liking. It should be quite dry but not sticking to the pan. Garnish with fresh coriander leaves and serve.

Tikka Ceylon Curry

Ceylon curries at the restaurant contain chilli for heat, coconut for creamy mildness and lemon for tart contrast. Delicious.

Serves 4

4 tablespoons water

1½ oz (40 g) block creamed coconut

2 tablespoons ghee or oil

2–3 garlic cloves, finely chopped

1½ lb (675 g) cooked (hot or cold) tikka of your choice (tikka meat, poultry, fish or vegetables from chapters 2–5)

2 tablespoons mild curry paste (page 21)

16 fl oz (450 g) cooked tikka/tandoori masala curry gravy (page 80)

2 tablespoons desiccated coconut

juice of one lemon

0–2 fresh green chillies

salt to taste

desiccated coconut, to garnish

Spices
1 teaspoon cummin seeds

½ teaspoon fennel seeds

1 Heat the water in a saucepan. Add the creamed coconut block and allow to melt until creamy and bubbling.

2 Heat the ghee or oil in a karahi or wok and stir-fry the **spices** for 30 seconds. Add the garlic and stir-fry for a further 30 seconds.

3 Add the tikka ingredient of your choice and briskly stir-fry for 2 minutes. Add and stir-fry the curry paste for a further minute.

4 Stir in the tikka/tandoori masala curry gravy and bring it to the simmer.

5 Add the melted coconut, the 2 tablespoons desiccated coconut, lemon juice, chillies and salt to taste. Simmer until it is cooked to your liking. Garnish with desiccated coconut and serve.

Tikka Dhansak

The original Dhansak is a Parsee dish in which meat is cooked in a purée of lentils and vegetables. The restaurants have simplified it by mixing cooked meat with cooked lentils. Here the main ingredient is cooked tikka-style to create a very tasty combination.

Serves 4

1 tablespoon ghee or vegetable oil

2–3 garlic cloves, finely chopped

1½ tablespoons mild curry paste (page 21)

1½ lb (675 g) cooked (hot or cold) tikka of your choice (tikka meat, poultry, fish or vegetables from chapters 2–5)

16 oz (450 g) cooked tikka/tandoori masala curry gravy (page 80)

2 oz (50 g) cooked red lentils

1 tablespoon white granulated sugar

2 teaspoons vinegar (any type)

2 teaspoons garam masala (page 18)

0–3 fresh green chillies, finely chopped

salt to taste

some fresh coriander leaves or chopped red pepper to garnish

Spices
1 teaspoon cummin seeds

½ teaspoon fenugreek seeds

1 Heat the ghee or oil in a karahi or wok. Stir-fry the spices for 30 seconds then add the garlic and stir-fry for a further 30 seconds. Add the mild curry paste and stir-fry for a further minute.

2 Add the tikka ingredient of your choice and briskly stir-fry it for about 2 minutes.

3 Add the tikka/tandoori masala curry gravy and bring it to the simmer.

4 When simmering, add the lentils, sugar, vinegar, garam masala and chillies and salt to taste. Simmer until it is cooked to your liking. Garnish with coriander leaves or chopped red pepper and serve.

Tikka Jal Frezi

This quick and easy stir-fry is now one of the most popular dishes at the curry house. It is even more popular given the tikka treatment.

Serves 4

1 tablespoon ghee or vegetable oil

2–3 garlic cloves, finely chopped

2 tablespoons red tandoori paste (page 24)

1 tablespoon green masala paste (page 22)

4 oz (110 g) onion, thinly sliced

1½ lb (675 g) cooked (hot or cold) tikka of your choice (tikka meat, fish, poultry or vegetables from chapters 2–5)

½ red pepper, cut into small diamond shapes

½ green pepper, cut into small diamond shapes

1–4 fresh green chillies, sliced

2–4 tablespoons fresh coriander, finely chopped

squeeze of lemon juice

sprinkles of garam masala (page 18)

fresh coriander leaves to garnish

Spices

1½ teaspoons cummin seed

½ teaspoon lovage seed

½ teaspoon coriander seed

1 Heat the oil in a karahi or wok. Stir-fry the spices for 30 seconds then add the garlic and stir-fry for a further 30 seconds. Add the tandoori and green masala pastes and stir-fry for a further minute. Add the onion and stir-fry for 3 more minutes.

2   Add the tikka ingredient of your choice and briskly stir-fry it for
    about 2 minutes, adding a little water to keep things moving.

3   Add the peppers, chillies, chopped coriander, lemon juice and
    garam masala and simmer until it is cooked to your liking. Salt to
    taste. It should be quite dry. Garnish with coriander leaves and
    serve.

Tikka Kofta Curry

Koftas are small minced-meat balls cooked in a curry gravy. These
ones use sheek kebab mixture and are particularly tasty.

Serves 4

1¼ lb (560 g) uncooked
sheek kebab mixture (page
36)

1 tablespoon ghee or
vegetable oil

2–3 garlic cloves, finely
chopped

1 tablespoon mild curry
paste (page 21)

16 oz (450 g) tikka/tandoori
masala curry gravy (page 80)

1 tablespoon tomato purée

6 oz (175 g) tinned
tomatoes, strained

1 teaspoon white
granulated sugar

½ teaspoon dried
fenugreek leaves

salt to taste

some fresh coriander
leaves to garnish

1   Divide the sheek kebab mixture into four equal parts. From each
    part roll 6 small balls (koftas).

2   Preheat the oven to 375°F/190°C/Gas 5. Put the 24 koftas on an
    oven tray and bake them for 15 minutes.

3   Heat the ghee or oil in a karahi or wok and stir-fry the garlic for 30
    seconds. Add the mild curry paste and stir-fry for a further minute.

4   Add the koftas and briskly stir-fry for about 2 minutes. Add the
    tikka/tandoori masala curry gravy and bring to the simmer.

5 Add the tomato purée, strained tomatoes, sugar and fenugreek, and salt to taste. Simmer for about 5 minutes or until it is cooked to your liking. Garnish with coriander leaves.

Tikka Korma Curry

'Korma' describes a method of slow cooking rather than the heat level of a particular dish. In Kashmir they produce a red korma bursting with red Kashmiri chillies! However, this restaurant version uses aromatic spices, cream, milk and saffron to produce a mild and creamy curry.

Serves 4

1 tablespoon ghee or vegetable oil

2–3 garlic cloves, finely chopped

1½ teaspoons mild curry paste (page 21)

1½ lb (675 g) cooked (hot or cold) tikka of your choice (tikka meat, fish, poultry or vegetables from chapters 2–5)

8 oz (225 g) tikka/tandoori masala curry gravy (page 80)

2 oz (50 g) coconut milk powder

5 fl oz (150 ml) thick double cream

1 teaspoon sugar

20 whole fried almonds

20–25 saffron strands

salt to taste

some fresh coriander leaves, to garnish

Spices
2 bay leaves

2 inch (5 cm) piece cassia bark

4–6 green cardamom pods

4–6 cloves

1 Heat the ghee or oil in a karahi or wok. Stir-fry the spices for 30 seconds then add the garlic and stir-fry for a further 30 seconds. Add the mild curry paste and stir-fry for a further minute.

2 Add the tikka ingredient of your choice and briskly stir-fry it for

about 3 minutes. Add the tikka/tandoori masala curry gravy and bring it to the simmer.

3 Stir in the coconut milk powder, cream, sugar, almonds, saffron and salt to taste. Simmer until it is cooked to your liking. Garnish with coriander leaves and serve.

Tikka Moghlai Curry

Also called *Mughlai*, this curry is named after the celebrated and very rich Moghul emperors. It is a creation of the Indian restaurant and is indeed opulent and very rich, with a sauce of ghee, cream, nuts and yoghurt in which tikka ingredients are combined.

~~~~~~~~~~~~~~~~

Serves 4

1 tablespoon ghee or vegetable oil

2–3 garlic cloves, finely chopped

1 tablespoon mild curry paste (page 21)

3½ oz (100 g) raw cashew nuts

5 fl oz (150 ml) single cream

4 tablespoons Greek yoghurt

8oz (225 g) tikka/tandoori masala curry gravy (page 80)

1½ lb (675 g) cooked (hot or cold) tikka of your choice (tikka meat, poultry, fish or vegetables from chapters 2–5)

20 strands saffron

1 tablespoon fresh coriander, finely chopped

2 tablespoons dehydrated onion flakes

salt to taste

melted ghee, to garnish

fresh coriander leaves, to garnish

almond flakes, to garnish

Spices

2 brown cardamom pods

2 star anises

1 teaspoon aniseed

1 teaspoon sesame seeds

~~~~~~~~~~~~~~~~

1 Heat the oil in a karahi or wok. Stir-fry the **spices** for 30 seconds then add the garlic and stir-fry for a further 30 seconds. Add the mild curry paste and stir-fry for a further minute.

2 Mix the nuts, cream and yoghurt together in a blender to form a fine paste that can be poured. Add a little water if needed.

3 Add the nuts, cream and yoghurt paste and the tikka/tandoori masala curry gravy to the karahi or wok. Bring it to the simmer.

4 Add the tikka ingredient of your choice and briskly stir-fry it for about 3 minutes, or until hot right through.

5 Add the saffron, chopped coriander and onion flakes and salt to taste.

6 Drizzle with a little melted ghee, and garnish with coriander leaves and almond flakes.

Tikka Patia Curry

The original Patia curry came from Persia via the Parsee (ex-Persian) community who now live in Bombay. It is a rich deep-red colour and is sweet and savoury and hottish – typical Parsee flavours.

Serves 4

1 tablespoon ghee or vegetable oil

2–3 garlic cloves, finely chopped

2 teaspoons paprika

1–2 teaspoons chilli powder

2 tablespoons mild curry paste (page 21)

1½ lb (675 g) cooked (hot or cold) tikka of your choice (tikka meat, poultry, fish or vegetables from chapters 2–5)

8 fl oz (225 ml) tikka/tandoori masala curry gravy (page 80)

1 tablespoon tomato purée

2–3 tomatoes, finely chopped

½ red pepper, very finely chopped

2 teaspoons brown sugar

1 tablespoon vinegar (any type)

salt to taste

some fresh coriander leaves to garnish

1   Heat the ghee or oil in a karahi or wok. Stir-fry the garlic, paprika and chilli powder for 30 seconds. Add the mild curry paste and stir-fry for a further minute.

2   Add your tikka ingredient and stir-fry for 2 minutes.

3   Stir in the tikka/tandoori masala curry gravy and tomato purée. Add the fresh tomatoes, red pepper, sugar and vinegar and simmer for at least 5 minutes more until it is cooked to your liking. Salt to taste and garnish with coriander leaves.

Tikka Rhogan Josh

This recipe is based (very loosely) on an authentic Kashmir dish from Moghul times.

~~~~~~~~~~~~~~~~~~~~~~~~~~

Serves 4

1 tablespoon ghee or vegetable oil

2–3 garlic cloves, finely chopped

1 teaspoon mild curry paste (page 21)

1½ lb (675 g) cooked (hot or cold) tikka of your choice (tikka meat, poultry, fish or vegetable from chapters 2–5)

16 oz (450 g) tikka/tandoori masala curry gravy (page 80)

1 tablespoon tomato purée

2 tablespoons ground almonds

1 red pepper, cut into diamonds

2 oz (50 g) fresh beetroot, peeled and shredded

1 tablespoon chopped fresh coriander leaves

salt to taste

fresh coriander leaves to garnish

Spices
6 cloves

2 bay leaves

2 inch (5 cm) piece cassia bark

2 brown cardamom pods

4 green cardamom pods

½ teaspoon black cummin seeds

½ teaspoon paprika

~~~~~~~~~~~~~~~~~~~~~~~~~~

1 Heat the oil in a karahi or wok. Stir-fry the **spices** for 30 seconds then add the garlic and stir-fry for a further 30 seconds. Add the mild curry paste and stir-fry for a further minute.

2 Add the tikka ingredient of your choice and briskly stir-fry it for about 3 minutes.

3 Add the tikka/tandoori masala curry gravy and bring it to the simmer.

4 Add the tomato purée, almonds, pepper, beetroot, chopped coriander and salt to taste. Simmer until it is cooked to your liking. Garnish with coriander leaves and serve.

Tikka Sag Gosht

This combination of tastes – meat and spinach (*sag*) with savoury spices – creates another typical authentic dish from the Punjab region.

Serves 4

2–3 tablespoons ghee or corn oil

3–6 garlic cloves, finely chopped

8 oz (225 g) onion, very finely chopped

3–4 tablespoons mild curry paste (page 21)

1 lb (450 g) fresh spinach leaves, or 8 oz (225 g) frozen spinach leaves, thawed

8 oz (225 g) tikka/tandoori masala curry gravy (page 80)

1 lb (450 g) cooked (hot or cold) meat tikka (see page 31)

1 tablespoon garam masala (page 18)

1 tablespoon very finely chopped fresh coriander leaves

salt to taste

Spices

2 teaspoons white cummin seeds

1 teaspoon black mustard seeds

1 teaspoon yellow mustard powder

½ teaspoon ground cinnamon

1   Heat the ghee or oil in a karahi or wok on high heat, then stir-fry the **spices** for 20 seconds. Add the garlic and continue stir-frying for a further 30 seconds.

2   Reduce the heat and add the onion. Stir-fry for 10 minutes, until the onion becomes translucent and begins to brown.

3   Add the mild curry paste. Raise the heat, and bring to a brisk sizzle, stir-frying as needed for about 5 minutes. Add the spinach and the gravy, and simmer, stirring, on a lower heat for about 10 minutes.

4   Add the meat tikka and simmer for about 5 minutes, adding a little water if required. When cooked to your liking, add the garam masala, fresh coriander leaves and salt to taste. Simmer for 5 minutes more, then serve.

Tikka Vindaloo Curry

Vindaloo is the archetypal curry house hot curry. As well as chilli powder this tikka version contains fresh red or green chillies and potatoes.

Serves 4

1 tablespoon ghee or vegetable oil

2–4 teaspoons chilli powder

2–3 garlic cloves, finely chopped

2 tablespoons mild curry paste (page 21)

1½ lb (675 g) cooked (hot or cold) tikka of your choice (tikka meat, poultry, fish or vegetables from chapters 2–5)

16 oz (450 g) tikka/tandoori masala curry gravy (page 80)

3–6 fresh red or green chillies, chopped

4–6 1½ inch/3.75 cm pieces cooked potato

2 teaspoons fenugreek leaf

salt to taste

some fresh coriander leaves to garnish

1 Heat the ghee or oil in a karahi or wok. Stir-fry the chilli powder for 30 seconds then add the garlic and stir-fry for a further 30 seconds. Add the mild curry paste and stir-fry for a further minute.

2 Add the tikka ingredient of your choice and briskly stir-fry it for about 2 minutes.

3 Add the tikka/tandoori masala curry gravy and bring it to the simmer.

4 Add the chillies, the potato, the fenugreek and salt to taste, and simmer until it is cooked to your liking. Garnish with coriander leaves and serve.

CHAPTER 8

Rice, Breads and Snacks

Traditionally tandoori and tikka dishes are accompanied with chutneys (see chapter 9) and naan bread, rather than rice. Rice was not indigenous to the mountainous area where tandoori and tikka evolved, but there is no reason why it should not be served with any of the recipes in this book.

I'd like to draw your attention to the especially excellent and very popular Tikka Biriani (page 110) which can be served with naan bread and chutneys for a satisfying meal. As well as a basic naan bread I've also included some unusual variations with which to ring the changes. And talking of change, try the fabulous Tandoori Pizza (page 116). It makes a great snack, anytime.

Other tasty snack recipes include Tandoori Scrambled Eggs (page 119) and some sandwich ideas.

Plain Boiled Rice

~~~~~~~~~~~~~~~~~~~~~~~~~~~

Serves 4 (makes 4 portions)

10 oz (300 g) Basmati rice

3 pints (1.75 litres) water

~~~~~~~~~~~~~~~~~~~~~~~~~~~

1 Pick through the rice to remove grit and impurities.

2 Put the water in a 4 or 5 pint (2 or 3 litre) pan. It is not necessary to salt it. Bring to the boil.

3 While the water is heating up, rinse the rice briskly with fresh cold water until most of the starch is washed out and the water runs clear. Boil a kettle of water and run this through the rice at the final rinse to minimise the temperature reduction of the boiling water in the pan when you put the rice into it.

4 When the water is boiling properly, put the rice into the pan. Start timing. Put the lid on the pan until the water comes back to the boil, then remove the lid. It takes 8–10 minutes from the start. Stir frequently.

5 After about 6 minutes, taste a few grains. As soon as the centre is no longer brittle but still has a good *al dente* bite to it, drain off the water. The rice should seem slightly undercooked.

6 Shake off all the excess water, then place the strainer on a dry tea towel which will help remove the last of the water.

7 After a minute place the rice in a warmed serving dish. You can serve it now or, preferably, put it into a very low oven or warming drawer for at least 30 minutes. As it dries, the grains will separate and become fluffy. It can be held in the warmer for up to 90 minutes. Just before serving, fluff up the rice with a fork to aerate it and release the steam.

Note: You can allow the rice to go cold after stage 7, and reheat it when required by quickly stir-frying it in a wok without any oil. It can also be frozen.

Fried Pullao Rice

There is a simple method for making tasty pullao rice out of plain boiled rice.

~~~~~~~~~~~~~~~~~~~~~~~~~~~~~~~~~~~~

Serves 4

1 tablespoon butter ghee or vegetable ghee

10 oz (300 g) Basmati rice, cooked and dried following the previous recipe

flakes of coconut, to garnish

Spices
1 teaspoon fennel seeds

½ teaspoon green cardamom seeds

½ teaspoon black cummin seeds

2 star anise

2 inch (5 cm) piece cassia bark

2 or 3 bay leaves

2 or 3 cloves

~~~~~~~~~~~~~~~~~~~~~~~~~~~~~~~~~~~~

1   Heat the ghee in a karahi or wok and stir-fry the spices for about 30 seconds.

2   Lower the heat, add the cooked rice and briskly stir-fry until it is hot enough to eat. If the heat is too high the rice will stick and burn. Garnish with the coconut flakes and serve at once.

Jeera Mattar Pullao

A colourful variation of the above recipe is easily created by adding the following ingredients to the cooked rice.

~~~~~~~~~~~~~~~~~~~~~~~~~~~~~~~~~~~~

1 tablespoon fried dehydrated onion flakes and 1 tablespoon mild curry paste (see page 21)

or
1 tablespoon red tandoori paste (see page 24) and 20–25 saffron strands

2 oz (50 g) cooked peas

~~~~~~~~~~~~~~~~~~~~~~~~~~~~~~~~~~~~

Pea-Fried Pullao

Basmati rice spiced with cummin seeds and saffron, and punctuated with green peas. It tastes as good as it looks.

Serves 4

8–12 oz (225–350 g) **Basmati rice**

2 tablespoons milk

20–25 saffron strands

2 tablespoons butter ghee

1 tablespoon onion in long thin strips

2 teaspoons cummin seeds

1 tablespoon mild curry paste (optional, page 21)

3 oz (75 g) cooked peas

salt to taste

1 Prepare and cook the rice by the method on page 107.

2 Warm but don't boil the milk, and put the saffron into it. After 10 minutes press the saffron to help it exude its colour.

3 As soon as the rice has begun to boil, heat the ghee in a karahi or wok. Stir-fry the onion until it crisps up (about 5 minutes). Add the cummin seeds and the curry paste as an optional extra.

4 When the rice is cooked place it in a warming pan. Add the stir-fry and the peas carefully so as not to break the rice grains.

5 Pour the saffron milk over the rice. Do not stir the rice.

6 Put the lid on the pan and place it into a warmer, or the lowest your oven will go. Leave it there for a minimum of 30 minutes, stirring after that time. Salt to taste. It can be held in the warmer for longer if you wish.

Tikka Biriani

The traditional biriani originated in Iran and is an oven-cooked rice dish. The tandoori house version is simpler – add tikka meat or chicken (or in fact any tikka recipe) to Fried Pullao Rice (page 108) and stir-fry. It is served with a substantial amount of garnish and can be accompanied with tikka/tandoori masala curry gravy. And of course, it is quite delicious.

Serves 4

2 tablespoons butter ghee or vegetable ghee

1–2 teaspoons desiccated coconut (optional)

1 full recipe of cooked tikka, for example 12 oz (350 g) cooked chicken tikka pieces (page 52)

10 oz (300 g) plain Basmati rice, cooked and dried (page 107)

Spices
1 teaspoon fennel seeds

½ teaspoon green cardamom seeds

½ teaspoon black cummin seeds

2 star anise

2 inch (5 cm) piece cassia bark

2 or 3 bay leaves

2 or 3 cloves

Garnish
(use all or some of these)

a knob of ghee

fried almonds, cashews and/or pistachios

fresh coconut flakes

20–30 saffron strands

fresh coriander and/or mint leaves, chopped

fried crispy brown onion slices

1   Heat the ghee in a karahi or wok and stir-fry the **spices** for about 30 seconds.

2   Add the coconut and the cooked chicken tikka pieces, plus any spare marinade. When sizzling and hot right through, add the cooked rice and stir-fry until the rice is also hot enough to eat.

3 Garnish elaborately and serve with a portion of tikka/tandoori masala curry gravy (see page 80), chutney and naan bread.

Kebab Biriani

This is a variation of the tikka biriani, using sheek kebab (page 36) in place of cooked tikka pieces.

Follow the previous recipe exactly substituting chopped cooked sheek kebab for the tikkas.

Naan Bread

The traditional bread cooked in the tandoor is called naan. It is a flat leavened bread containing yeast to aerate it and make it puffy. Cooking naan in the tandoor cannot be bettered – the bread is pressed against the top inside wall of the oven and it cooks in just a few minutes. However, good results can be obtained with a conventional grill. The latest restaurant trend is to cook the largest possible naan. I heard one such described as a 'naan as large as an elephant's ear'. If you wish to do that, follow the recipe overleaf for karak naan. I also give simple naan variations. (See also page 3.)

~~~~~~~~~~~~~~~~~~~~~~

Makes 4 naan breads

2 oz (50 g) fresh yeast or 3 tablespoons yoghurt

lukewarm water

1½ lb (675 g) strong white flour

1 teaspoon wild onion seeds (optional)

melted butter ghee or vegetable oil

~~~~~~~~~~~~~~~~~~~~~~

1 Dissolve the fresh yeast in a little lukewarm water.

2 Put the flour in a warmed bowl, make a well in the centre and pour in the yeast or yoghurt. Mix together, adding enough lukewarm water to make a firm dough.

3 Remove from the bowl and knead on a floured board until well combined. Return to the bowl and leave in a warm place for a couple of hours to rise.

4   Your dough, when risen, should have doubled in size. It should be bubbly, stringy and elastic. When it is, add the seeds and knock back the dough by kneading it down to its original size.

5   Divide the dough into four equal parts. On a floured work surface, roll out each piece into a tear-drop shape at least ¼ inch (5 mm) thick.

6   Preheat the grill to three-quarters heat, cover the rack pan with foil and set it in the midway position.

7   Put the naan on to the foil and grill it. Watch it cook (it can easily burn). As soon as the first side develops brown patches, remove it from the grill.

8   Turn it over and brush the uncooked side with a little melted ghee. Return it to the grill and cook until it is sizzling, then remove.

9   Cook the other three naan in the same way and serve at once.

Karak Naan

The karak naan first appeared in Birmingham's balti houses, who seem to delight in competing with each other to produce the largest possible naan. I've seen one 2 feet by 3 feet (60 × 90 cm). Also called *kharri jandala*, or simply, the family naan, these huge specimens are now appearing at tandoori houses. The size you can make at home is limited by the size of your grill pan and oven.

To make one karak naan, simply follow the previous naan recipe, but use all the dough to roll out one large tear-drop shape. It will be about 20 × 12 inches (50 × 30 cm) and will be quite difficult to handle. Place it on a foil-lined grill or oven pan and cook as in the previous recipe.

Naan E Panjagi

This is an Afghan variation of the standard naan. The rolled-out naan is decorated with a series of depressions made with your finger tips. (Long nails don't matter.) You should press quite hard to obtain the depressions.

Naan E Nakhooni

This is another Afghan variation. Here the rolled-out naan is indented all over with the impression of a builder's nail. Use one with a wide head such as clout used for plaster board. Push the length of the nail into the dough to create a 'T' shape. For heaven's sake, be careful! Only use one clean nail for the purpose, and be careful not to leave it embedded in the naan.

Naan Parakki

Naan parakki is a standard naan that is rolled out very thin so that it is crisp when cooked. Simply roll the naan out more thinly than usual. You are aiming for a long thin shape. It is easier to divide the dough into 8 rather than 4 pieces first. Be careful when grilling the naan – you want it crispy but watch that it doesn't burn.

Naan Roghani

Roghan in Iranian means ghee. (In Kashmir it means red.) Here we work ghee into the dough while it is being kneaded. Use 2 or 3 tablespoons of ghee. As an even tastier alternative, use two tablespoons ghee and two of butter. Never mind the calories! Roll out and grill as normal (page 111).

Tandoori Paste Naan

A really simple and very tasty variation on the naan bread theme. You can do this to any of the naan bread recipes in this book.

Simply smear red, green or raan tandoori paste or marinade on to the top side of the naan just prior to grilling.

Peshawari Naan

Peshawar is the nearest town in Pakistan to the Khyber Pass, and it is here that Tandoori cooking is said to have originated. This sweet naan, studded with almond flakes and sultanas, is very popular in tandoori restaurants.

~~~~~~~~~~

Makes 4 peshawari naans

2 oz (50 g) fresh yeast, or 3 tablespoons yoghurt

lukewarm water

1½ lb (675 g) strong white flour

2 teaspoons granulated sugar

1 teaspoon wild onion seeds (optional)

2–3 tablespoons flaked almonds

1–2 tablespoons sultanas

melted butter ghee or vegetable ghee

~~~~~~~~~~

1 Follow the naan bread recipe on page 111 to the end of stage 5.

2 Once you have rolled out the four naans, sprinkle half the almonds and sultanas over them and press in. Turn over and repeat with the other side.

3 Continue with the recipe on page 111 to the end.

Tandoori Keema Naan

Stuffed naan breads are extremely popular and worth the minimal effort to make. This one is stuffed with tandoori spice mince (in the form of the sheek kebab mix from page 36), which must be cooked first.

~~~~~~~~~~~~~~~~~~~~~~~~~

Makes 4 tandoori keema naan

approximately 6 oz (175 g) raw sheek kebabs mix (page 36)

a little vegetable oil or ghee

1 recipe naan bread dough (page 111)

2 tablespoons red tandoori paste (page 24)

~~~~~~~~~~~~~~~~~~~~~~~~~

1   Divide the kebab mix into four equal amounts, and flatten each into a thin 4 inch (10 cm) oval disc.

2   Fry the discs in a little oil or ghee in a flat pan until cooked. Allow to cool.

3   Make up the naan dough to the end of stage 5 on page 111, but roll out each piece into an oval nearly double the size of normal, so that it is about ⅛ inch (2.5 mm) thick.

4   Smear each oval with tandoori paste almost to the edges. Place a kebab disc on each oval, off-set to one side. Fold each oval over to enclose the paste and kebab disc, and press the edges together to seal. Carefully roll out to full size. Follow the remaining steps of the naan bread on page 111.

Kulcha Naan

Another stuffed naan recipe, this time using fried and cooled garlic and onion. Time is saved by using dried onion flakes.

~~~~~~~~~~~~~~~~~~~~~~~~~~~~~~~

Makes 4 kulcha naan

1 recipe naan bread dough (page 111)

1 tablespoon butter ghee or vegetable ghee

½ teaspoon white cummin seeds

4 garlic cloves, sliced

4 tablespoons dehydrated onion flakes

~~~~~~~~~~~~~~~~~~~~~~~~~~~~~~~

1   Prepare the naan bread to the end of stage 3 on page 111.

2   Heat the ghee in a karahi or wok.

3   Stir-fry the cummin seeds and garlic for 30 seconds, then add the onion.

4   Remove from the heat at once, stirring until it stops sizzling. Cool.

5   Add the cooled garlic and onion mixture to the dough when you knock it back, then proceed with the rest of the recipe on page 111.

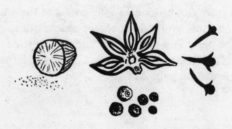

Ananas Naan

The stuffing for this variation is pineapple, which results in quite an interesting taste. For a sweet *and* hot version, add 2–3 finely chopped fresh red cayenne chillies too.

Makes 4 ananas naan

1 recipe naan bread dough (page 111)

4 oz (110 g) fresh or canned pineapple chunks, drained and coarsely chopped

1 Prepare the naan bread to the end of stage 3 on page 111.

2 Add the pineapple to the dough when you knock it back, then proceed with the rest of the recipe on page 111.

Tandoori Pizza

It sounds bizarre, perhaps, but what we have here is a combination of tikka and naan bread, the former being a topping for the latter. The result is delicious, if unconventional.

The topping here is a combination of prawns, chicken and strips of meat, which are stir-fried with tandoori paste, rather than marinated in it, to save time.

~~~~~~~~~~~~~~~~~

Makes 2 pizzas

Dough

1 oz (25 g) fresh yeast, or 1½ tablespoons yoghurt

lukewarm water

12 oz (350 g) strong white flour

1 teaspoon white sugar

1 tablespoon olive oil

Topping

2 tablespoons ghee

4 garlic cloves, thinly sliced

2 tablespoons red tandoori paste (page 24)

1 tablespoon green masala paste (page 22)

3 oz (75 g) small cooked prawns, shells off

3 oz (75 g) chicken breast, skinned and cut into strips ¼ inch (5 mm) thick and 2 inches (5 cm) long

2 oz (50 g) steak, cut into very thin slices about ½ inch (1.25 cm) by 2 inches (5 cm)

1 teaspoon mild curry paste (page 21)

1 oz (25 g) salami, chopped

1 tablespoon red pepper, chopped

1 tablespoon green pepper, chopped

2 oz (50 g) onion, chopped

1–4 fresh green or red chillies, sliced

1 tablespoon sundried tomatoes in olive oil, chopped

3–4 button mushrooms, chopped

3–4 canned anchovies, whole

1 tablespoon fresh coriander leaves

salt to taste

sesame oil for brushing

4 oz (100 g) Mozzarella cheese, chopped into cubes

Spices
½ teaspoon white cummin seeds

½ teaspoon black mustard seeds

½ teaspoon wild onion seeds

1 tablespoon dried oregano

½ teaspoon aniseed

~~~~~~~~~~~~~~~~~~~~~~~~~

1 Make the dough following the recipe for naan bread on page 111 to the end of stage 3, but adding the olive oil at stage 2.

2 Preheat the oven to 375°F/190°C/Gas 5.

3 Heat the ghee in your karahi or wok. Stir-fry the garlic for 30 seconds. Add the **spices** and stir-fry for 30 seconds more. Add the tandoori pastes and when sizzling add the prawns, chicken and meat. Stir-fry briskly for 5 minutes.

4 Mix in the remaining ingredients except the cheese, then remove from the heat and allow to cool for 5 or 10 minutes.

5 Knock back the dough by kneading it to its original size.

6 Choose an oven tray of about 14 × 8 inches (35.5 × 20 cm). Roll out the dough to a size that will fit the oven tray and gives you a thickness of at least ¼ inch (5 mm). Place the pizza on the tray, pressing it down with your fingers, and brush its top with sesame oil.

7 Leaving a ¾ inch (2 cm) margin all around the edge of the dough, spoon the stir-fry evenly over the top. Scatter with the cubes of Mozarella.

8 Put the pizza into the centre of the oven and bake for about 10–15 minutes. As ovens vary, check it after 10 minutes and judge whether it needs more baking time. (The tikka ingredients will be cooked and it is the bread which you are judging.) Serve piping hot.

Tandoori Scrambled Eggs

This is an ingenious and simple recipe that makes an extremely tasty snack at any time. Try it in a sandwich.

~~~~~~~~~~~~~~~~~~~~~~~~~~~~~

Serves 2 as a snack

4 large eggs

2 teaspoons cream

1 teaspoon butter

½ teaspoon cummin seeds, roasted

1 teaspoon red tandoori paste (page 24)

salt to taste

chilli powder to taste

mustard cress to garnish

~~~~~~~~~~~~~~~~~~~~~~~~~~~~~

1 Lightly beat the eggs with a fork, then beat in the cream.

2 Heat the butter in a small saucepan, then pour in the eggs. Immediately add the cummin and the tandoori paste and with minimal heat, stir until the eggs are solid but not dry.

3 Sprinkle with salt and chilli powder to taste. Garnish and serve hot or cold.

Tikka Sandwiches

I mentioned in the previous recipe that tandoori scrambled eggs makes a great sandwich filler. So too does any tikka recipe from this book. It's a great way to use up cold leftovers. As a matter of interest, chicken tikka are the top-selling supermarket sandwiches.

You'll come up with many ideas for sandwich fillers. Simply chop the cold cooked tikkas to make them more manageable. Put onion salad (page 124) in the sandwich as well, or a bed of salad.

Sheek Kebab Torpedos

And here's a variant. Use halved French bread. First spread it with a little mild curry paste, then put in a bed of salad. Finally insert a sheek kebab (page 36). Grrreatt!

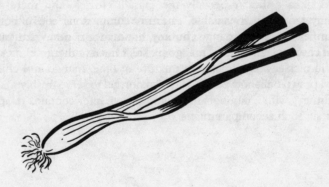

CHAPTER 9

Fresh Chutneys

Any bottled Indian chutneys and pickles go well with tandoori and tikka dishes, especially the masala curries, and there are many good brands available. The most common varieties of bottle chutneys are sweet mango chutney, hot mango chutney, fruit and nut chutney, lime pickle, mango pickle, brinjal (aubergine) pickle, chilli pickle, mixed pickle (a mixture of lime, mango and chilli) and prawn balichow pickle. It is also normal to serve freshly made chutneys with a tandoori meal, and this chapter contains recipes for six such accompaniments.

Tandoori Chutney (Mint Raita)

This simple-to-make chutney/raita is based on yoghurt, with a wee bit of spicing.

〜〜〜〜〜〜〜〜

Enough for 4

5 oz (150 ml) Greek yoghurt

1 tablespoon chopped fresh mint (if available)

1 teaspoon bottled vinegared mint

½ teaspoon garam masala

〜〜〜〜〜〜〜〜

Simply mix the ingredients together, chill and serve.

Tandoori Chutney – Red Variation

Follow the previous recipe, but add ½–1 teaspoon red tandoori paste (page 24) to the mixture, stirring it in well.

Tandoori Chutney – Green Variation

Follow the recipe for tandoori chutney – mint raita (above), but add ½–1 teaspoon green masala paste (page 22) to the mixture, stirring it in well.

Tandoori Chutney – Yellow Variation

Follow the recipe for tandoori chutney (above), but add ½–1 teaspoon mild curry paste (page 21) and about ⅓ teaspoon turmeric to the mixture, stirring them in well.

Onion Salad (Cachumber)

A splendid and healthy accompaniment to a tandoori meal. If you want the onions to be translucent (the way most restaurants serve it), cover and leave the mixture in the fridge overnight, or longer.

Enough for 4

½ **Spanish onion, thinly sliced**

1 **teaspoon red pepper, finely chopped**

1 **teaspoon green pepper, finely chopped**

⅓ **teaspoon dried mint**

1 **teaspoon fresh coriander leaves, chopped**

Mix everything together and serve.

Cachumber Raita

This is a combination of salad and yoghurt. Simply combine any of the tandoori chutney recipes on page 121 with the previous onion salad recipe. Chill and serve.

Note: This larger quantity will keep covered in the fridge for 3–4 days.

Appendix 1
THE CURRY CLUB

Pat Chapman always had a deep-rooted interest in spicy food, curry in particular, and over the years he built up a huge pool of information which he felt could be usefully passed on to others. He conceived the idea of forming an organisation for this purpose.

Since it was founded in January 1982, **The Curry Club** has built up a membership of several thousands. We have a marchioness, some lords and ladies, knights a-plenty, a captain of industry or two, generals, admirals and air marshals (not to mention a sprinkling of ex-colonels), and we have celebrity names – actresses, politicians, rock stars and sportsmen. We have an airline (Air India), a former R.N. warship (HMS *Hermes*) and a hotel chain (the Taj group).

We have 15 members whose name is Curry or Currie, 20 called Rice, and several with the name Spice or Spicer, Cook, Fry, Frier, or Fryer, and one Boiling. We have a Puri (a restaurant owner), a Paratha and a Nan, a good many Mills and Millers, one Dal and a Lentil, an Oiler, a Gee (but no Ghee), and a Butter but not Marj (several Majories though, and a Majoram and a Minty). We also have several Longs and Shorts, Thins and Broads, one Fatt and one Wide, and a Chilley and a Coole.

We have members on every continent, including a good number of Asian members, but by and large the membership is a typical cross-section of the Great British Public, ranging in age from teenage to dotage, and in occupation from refuse collectors to receivers, high-street traders to high-court judges, tax inspectors to taxi drivers. There are students and pensioners, millionaires and unemployed ... thousands of people who have just one thing in common – a love of curry and spicy foods.

Members receive a bright and colourful magazine four times a year, which has regular features on curry and the curry lands. It includes news items, recipes, reports on restaurants, picture features and contributions from members and professionals alike. The information is largely concerned with curry, but by popular demand it now includes regular input on other exotic and spicy cuisines such as those of the Middle East and China. We have produced a wide selection of publications, including the books listed on page ii, all published by Piatkus.

Obtaining the ingredients required for Indian, Oriental and Middle Eastern cooking can be difficult, but The Curry Club makes it easy, with a comprehensive range of Curry Club products, including spice mixes, chutneys, pickles, papadoms, sauces and curry pastes. These are available from major food stores and specialist delicatessens up and down the country. If they are not stocked near you, there is the Club's well-established and efficient mail-order service. Hundreds of items are stocked, including spices, pickles, pastes, dry foods, tinned food, gift items, publications and specialist kitchen and tableware.

On the social side, the Club holds residential weekend cookery courses and gourmet nights to selected restaurants.

Top of the list is our regular Curry Club Gourmet trip to India and other spicy countries. We take a small group of curry enthusiasts to the chosen country and tour the incredible sights, in between sampling the delicious foods of each region.

If you would like more information about The Curry Club, write (enclosing a SAE) to: **The Curry Club, PO Box 7, Haslemere, Surrey GU27 1EP.**

Appendix 2
THE STORE CUPBOARD

Here is a workable list of items that you will need to make the recipes in this book, subdivided into essential and non-essential. The essential items appear again and again in the recipes, the non-essential appear only in one or two. This list may look a bit formidable but remember, once you have the items in stock they will last for some time. I have listed in metric only as most of the packaging these days *is* metric only.

I have given the ethnic name for each spice in italics, which may be useful if you are buying from Asian food stores. I have never found a store that stocks everything. However, all items listed are available, in the quantities stated, by post from The Curry Club (see Appendix 1 for address).

ESSENTIAL WHOLE SPICES

Aniseeds (*Soonf chotti*) 50 g
Bay leaves (*Tej patia*) 4 g
Cardamom, black or brown (*Elaichi motti*) 15 g
Cardamom, white or green (*Elaichi chota/hari*) 15 g
Cassia bark (*Dalchini*) 6 g
Chillies, red (*Lal mirch*) 5 g
Cloves (*Lavang*) 13 g
Coriander seeds (*Dhania*) 13 g
Cummin seeds, white (*Jeera safed*) 18 g
Curry leaves, dry (*Neempatta* or *Kari phulia*) 4 g
Fennel seeds (*Soonf*) 15 g
Fenugreek leaves, dry (*Tej methi kasoori*) 4 g
Mustard seeds (*Rai*) 35 g
Peppercorns, black (*Kala mirch*) 2 g
Sesame seeds, white (*Til*) 29 g
Wild onion seeds (*Kalonji*) 28 g

NON-ESSENTIAL WHOLE SPICES

Cummin seeds, black (*kala* or *Shahli jeera*) 20 g
Fenugreek seeds (*Methi dana*) 36 g
Lovage seeds (*Ajowan*) 50 g
Panch phoran (*Panch phoran*) 20 g
Saffron stamens (*Zafraan* or *Kesar*) ½ g
Star aniseed (*Chakriphool*) 12 g

GROUND SPICES

Black pepper (*Kala mirch*) 22 g
Chilli powder (*Lal mirch*) 20 g
Coriander (*Dhania*) 16 g
Cummin (*Jeera*) 16 g
Mango Powder (*Am chur*) 25 g
Paprika (*Paprika*) 20 g
Turmeric (*Huldi*) 21 g

ESSENTIAL DRY FOODS

Basmati rice (*Basmati*) 500 g
Coconut Powder (*Koprai* or *Narial*) 50 g
Gram flour (*Besan*) 500 g
Red lentils (*Masoor dal*) 500 g

NON-ESSENTIAL DRY FOODS

Food colouring powder, red (beetroot powder)
25 g

Food colouring powder, yellow (anatto)   25 g

Nuts (raw and shelled) – Almond, whole (*Badan*)   50 g

Cashew (*Kaju*)   100 g

Pistachio (*Pista*)   100 g